THE SCIENCE-BACKED
MEDITERRANEAN
DIET COOKBOOK
FOR BEGINNERS

Rejuvenate Your Health with 150 Easy and Quick 30-Minute
Delicious Recipes, a 30-Day Meal Plan with Shopping Lists,
and 100 Lifestyle Tips

Elena Florenz

TABLE OF CONTENTS

41

Chapter 8

Soups

47

Chapter 9

Salads

54

Chapter 10

Vegetables

67

Chapter 11

Whole grains, Beans, and Pasta

76

Chapter 12

Fish and Seafood

INTRODUCTION

The journey to better health is one that is deeply personal and profoundly transformative. I wrote this book with a goal of providing you with scientifically backed information combined with practical, useful tools to aid you on your path to rejuvenation and well-being.

This book, **"The Science-Backed Mediterranean Diet Cookbook for Beginners: Rejuvenate Your Health with 150 Easy and Quick 30-Minute Delicious Recipes, a 30-Day Meal Plan with Shopping Lists, and 100 Lifestyle Tips by Elena Florenz,"** is a comprehensive guide that will lead you toward a healthier lifestyle. My intention is to help you navigate the sometimes intricate maze of dietary changes and lifestyle adjustments needed to improve your overall health. I have included as much information as possible to help you understand the science behind the Mediterranean diet, including its origins and its well-established benefits supported by extensive research in nutrition and health sciences.

We all owe it to ourselves to address the health issues that can be mitigated through proper nutrition and lifestyle choices. In a world where health challenges are increasingly common, you need to learn how to be your own best advocate for well-being. This book delves into the essence of what it means to rejuvenate your health through dietary changes while exploring the practical aspects of implementing these changes in your daily life.

Why should you follow this guide? Because the Mediterranean diet is not just a diet; it is a lifestyle that has been shown to reduce the risk of chronic diseases, improve heart health, and promote longevity. *How does this book help you achieve this?* By providing you with 150 easy and quick recipes that can be prepared in 30 minutes or less, ensuring that even the busiest individuals can incorporate healthy meals into their routine. Additionally, the 30-day meal plan with shopping lists takes the guesswork out of meal preparation, making it easier for you to stay on track. *When should you start?* Now is the perfect time to begin your journey toward better health. The sooner you start, the sooner you will experience the benefits.

To enrich your culinary experience further, consider these bonus books: "Lavish Dishes for the Weekends & Familial Gatherings: 25 Classic Mediterranean Recipes to Eat, Cook & Partake Together," elevating your repertoire for special occasions and gatherings. Additionally, "Spices and Herbs in Mediterranean Cuisine" provides a deep dive into the aromatic elements that define Mediterranean dishes. And don't miss our latest addition, "Mediterranean Smoothies," featuring refreshing blends to enhance your well-being and bring vibrant flavors to your daily routine. Together, these resources aim to elevate the joy of shared meals with loved ones, celebrating good health and delicious flavors.

With clear guidance, delicious recipes, and actionable 100 lifestyle tips aimed at promoting overall physical and emotional health, this cookbook is designed to help you mitigate health issues by offering a practical, science-backed approach to nutrition. I hope you will find that rejuvenating your health has never been more achievable or enjoyable.

CHAPTER 1

DISCOVERING THE MEDITERRANEAN DIET

Embark on a vibrant lifelong journey to rejuvenate your health through ancient wisdom and modern health benefits.

For those accustomed to meat-centric diets, the absence of traditional staples might seem daunting. But fear not, for the Mediterranean Diet proves that healthy eating can be both delicious and satisfying.

So join us as we embark on a culinary journey through the Mediterranean Diet. Let's explore the flavors, traditions, and health benefits that have made this way of eating a timeless treasure.

ORIGINS AND CULTURAL SIGNIFICANCE
Historical Context and Countries Involved

The Mediterranean Diet traces its roots back to the ancient civilizations that flourished around the Mediterranean basin—a geographical region encompassing coastal plains, rugged mountains, and fertile valleys. From the sun-kissed shores of Greece to the picturesque landscapes of Italy, Spain, and beyond, the diet evolved as a tapestry woven from diverse culinary traditions.

Throughout history, civilizations such as the Greeks, Romans, Phoenicians, Arabs, and Ottomans left an indelible mark on the culinary landscape of the Mediterranean. With each culture contributing unique ingredients, cooking techniques, and flavors, the diet became a reflection of the rich tapestry of Mediterranean life.

Evolution over Time

Over the centuries, the Mediterranean Diet underwent a fascinating evolution. Trade routes crisscrossing the sea brought new ingredients and cooking styles, enriching the culinary tapestry. Conquerors and colonizers

UNVEILING THE MEDITERRANEAN

Picture yourself strolling along the sun-drenched coastlines of the Mediterranean, from the quaint island towns like Lipari to bustling cities like Barcelona. The air is filled with the scent of fresh herbs, the laughter of locals, and the promise of culinary delights. In these vibrant locales, one thing remains constant—the Mediterranean Diet.

The Mediterranean Diet is not just a way of eating; it's a celebration of life itself. It's about embracing tradition and flavor, with plates brimming with colorful vegetables, succulent fruits, and the freshest seafood imaginable. Olive oil, the golden elixir, infuses every dish with its distinctive flavor.

Living the Mediterranean lifestyle means more than just following a set of dietary guidelines. It's deeply rooted in tradition and community. It's about savoring meals with loved ones, enjoying the bounty of nature, and feeling connected to the rhythms of the land and sea.

introduced exotic flavors and techniques, shaping the diet's development.

Despite these changes, the essence of the Mediterranean Diet—its focus on fresh, simple ingredients—remained unchanged. It became a delicious time capsule, preserving centuries of culinary wisdom and cultural heritage.

MEDITERRANEAN DIET HISTORICAL DEVELOPMENT TIMELINE

ANCIENT ORIGINS

The foundations of the Mediterranean diet can be traced back to ancient civilizations such as the Greeks and Romans, who relied heavily on foods like olive oil, grains, fruits, and vegetables.

EARLY INFLUENCES

The diet was further shaped by various cultural and historical influences, including trade with the Middle East and North Africa, which introduced spices, herbs, and grains like wheat and barley.

MIDDLE AGES

During the Middle Ages, the Mediterranean diet continued to evolve with the introduction of new foods such as citrus fruits, almonds, and spices brought by traders from Asia.

RENAISSANCE AND EXPLORATION

The Renaissance period saw a flourishing of culinary arts in the Mediterranean region, influenced by the explorations of new lands and the exchange of food cultures with the Americas.

20TH CENTURY RECOGNITION

The modern concept of the Mediterranean diet emerged in the mid-20th century when researchers began to study the dietary habits of Mediterranean populations, noting their lower rates of chronic diseases

1950S-1960S

The Seven Countries Study, led by Ancel Keys, provided key insights into the health benefits of the Mediterranean diet, leading to increased international interest and recognition.

1980S-PRESENT

Since the 1980s, numerous scientific studies have highlighted the health benefits of the Mediterranean diet, leading to its widespread adoption and promotion by health organizations worldwide.

CHAPTER 2

THE SCIENCE BEHIND THE MEDITERRANEAN DIET

In the art of nourishing the body, the Mediterranean diet is a delicate masterpiece infused with scientific evidence for optimal health and longevity.

WHY CHOOSE THE MEDITERRANEAN DIET?
Scientific Studies Supporting Its Health Benefits

Imagine this: a diet so good, it's like a shield for your heart and an all–rounded diet that can rejuvenate your overall health. That's the Mediterranean Diet for you. Packed with abundance of vibrant vegetables, succulent fruits, and the liquid gold of olive oil, it serves as a cornerstone for nourishing your body in myriad ways. Its rich variety of nutrients and antioxidants work synergistically to promote optimal health and vitality, making it a choice that extends far beyond any singular aspect of wellness. Here are some benefits as follows:

1. Heart Health:

The Mediterranean Diet stands as a beacon of heart health, backed by scientific evidence. Its rich array of fruits, vegetables, and olive oil, alongside the omega-3-packed fish, creates a protective shield for your cardiovascular system. According to American Heart Association, monounsaturated fats from olive oil and antioxidants from plant-based foods join forces to combat inflammation and oxidative stress, the primary culprits behind heart disease.

2. Managing Type 2 Diabetes

Research also suggests that the Mediterranean Diet effectively manages type 2 diabetes by focusing on whole grains, legumes, and fiber-rich foods, curbing blood sugar spikes and lowering rates of obesity and metabolic syndrome.

3. Reduced Cancer Risks

In addition, the Mediterranean Diet is associated with decreased risks of specific cancers, including breast and colorectal cancers. This is attributed to its abundance of plant-based foods packed with cancer-fighting vitamins, minerals, and phytochemicals.

4. Cognitive Enhancement

The Mediterranean Diet isn't just about the body; it's a boon for cognitive health too. According to a research of PJ Smith with antioxidants, omega-3s, and anti-inflammatory properties, it enhances brain function, reducing the risk of Alzheimer's and dementia with age.

5. Longevity: Nourishing Body and Soul

Picture a life brimming with vitality and zest, where age is merely a number. That's the promise of the Mediterranean Diet, dedicated to nourishing both body and soul for enduring well-being

6. Obesity: A Balanced Approach

Based on studies, the Mediterranean Diet offers a comprehensive method for managing weight. It goes beyond simply shedding pounds; it prioritizes nourishing the body for enduring health and happiness. What distinguishes the Mediterranean Diet in weight management is its emphasis on wholesome ingredients like fruits, vegetables, whole grains, and lean proteins, while minimizing processed foods and added sugars - promoting feelings of fullness and encouraging healthier eating habits. Additionally, the moderate consumption of healthy fats, mainly from sources like olive oil and nuts, helps regulate appetite and curb excessive eating.

COMPARISON WITH OTHER DIETARY APPROACHES

Contrasting with the Western Diet

When choosing diets, it's vital to compare approaches. Let's start with the Mediterranean Diet versus the Western diet. The Western diet, high in processed foods and red meat, poses cardiovascular risks. In contrast, the Mediterranean Diet focuses on healthful fats, plant-based foods, and moderate fish consumption. It prioritizes heart health with monounsaturated fats from olive oil, nuts, and avocados, offering a balanced alternative to the saturated fats in the Western diet.

Comparison with Trendy Diets

Furthermore, compared to trendy diets like Keto or Paleo, the Mediterranean Diet shines as a gold standard of balance and sustainability. Unlike quick-fix approaches, it prioritizes nourishing the body and soul with the flavors and traditions of the Mediterranean. By championing lean proteins and omega-3 fatty acids from fish such as salmon and tuna, it diverges from the emphasis on red meat.

Principles of the Diet

Let's take a journey to the lands bordering the Mediterranean Sea, where food isn't just sustenance; it's a way of life. Here, the Mediterranean Diet isn't just about what you eat; it's about how you nourish your body for optimal health.

MEDITERRANEAN DIET PYRAMID

Visualize a pyramid brimming with nutritional goodness, where plant-based foods form the sturdy foundation. Fruits, vegetables, whole grains, legumes, nuts, and seeds take center stage, offering a bounty of essential nutrients your body thrives on. At the pyramid's apex? A delicate balance of lean proteins and beneficial fats, including olive oil and omega-3s sourced from fish.

- **Percentages of Key Food Categories:** Visualize around 50-60% of your calories from carbs, 15-20% from protein, and 25-35% from fats, mostly the heart-loving kind from olive oil and fish.
- **Healthy Fats:** Say hello to the heroes of heart health, monounsaturated fats, found in olive oil, avocados, and nuts. They're like a shield against inflammation and champions for cognitive function.
- **Whole Grains:** These are the unsung heroes of the Mediterranean Diet, like barley, quinoa, and brown rice, packed with fiber and nutrients for a happy tummy.

MEDITERRANEAN DIET

CHAPTER 3

EMBRACING THE MEDITERRANEAN LIFESTYLE

Share a meal, share a story, and find joy in the simple moments. Relish the Mediterranean lifestyle, where every step is about making connections for your overall well-being.

EMOTIONAL AND MENTAL HEALTH BENEFITS OF MEDITERRANEAN LIFESTYLE

In Mediterranean towns, communal dining isn't merely about satisfying hunger; it's a cherished tradition that deeply nourishes emotional and mental well-being. Families and friends gather around tables laden with vibrant dishes, creating cherished moments that extend beyond mere nourishment. Research underscores the profound impact of communal dining on mental health and overall happiness. Frequent communal meals correlate with higher levels of happiness and life satisfaction, emphasizing its vital role in nurturing mental well-being.

Moreover, the Mediterranean diet, renowned for its physical health benefits, also positively impacts mood and emotional well-being. Rich in fruits, vegetables, whole grains, and lean meats, this diet is brimming with nutrients like omega-3 fatty acids and antioxidants that promote brain health and emotional resilience. Studies from Harvard University highlight the mood-enhancing effects of the Mediterranean diet, indicating a reduced risk of depression and anxiety among adherents.

In conclusion, the Mediterranean lifestyle offers myriad benefits for both body and mind. In accordance with research, by embracing healthy eating habits, participating in communal dining experiences, staying physically active, and nurturing meaningful relationships individuals can cultivate a life of greater happiness and fulfillment. Drawing inspiration from Mediterranean culture, they cherish the simple joys of life shared with loved ones, fostering joy, fortifying bonds, and instilling a sense of collective belonging and solidarity.

AUTHOR'S STORY: THE ART OF CONNECTION

In Sicily, where time seems to slow down and the sun casts a golden hue over cobblestone streets, a moment of pure connection unfolded. Walking together with a local friend, we were stopped by a neighbor. What began as a simple greeting turned into a heartfelt conversation that lasted for minutes. In that fleeting encounter, the profound importance of taking the time to say "hello" and the transformative power of human connection became evident.

Now, let's embark on a journey through the Mediterranean lifestyle, where each tip serves as a beacon of inspiration for infusing busy lives with the warmth, vitality, and sense of belonging that define this cherished way of living.

TIPS FOR EMBRACING THE MEDITERRANEAN LIFESTYLE

Incorporating the Mediterranean lifestyle into a modern, bustling life may initially seem daunting. However, with creativity and intentionality, it's entirely feasible. According to research by Cambridge University on Mediterranean diet, culture, and lifestyle, as well as findings from the Nutrition Journal and Behavior, here are 100 practical tips to seamlessly integrate the Mediterranean way of living into your daily routine.

Begin your day with a glass of water infused with lemon for hydration and a vitamin C boost.

1	Prioritize whole, minimally processed foods over packaged snacks and convenience meals.	2	Prepare traditional Mediterranean one-pot dishes like paella or shakshuka for convenience and rich flavor.
3	Grow your own Mediterranean herbs and vegetables like tomatoes, peppers, and eggplants to use in your cooking.	4	Create a mindful morning routine with gratitude journaling, and gentle stretching to start your day with clarity and purpose.
5	Make heart-healthy olive oil an important must-use ingredient in your cooking and salad dressings.	6	Occasionally dine at Mediterranean restaurants to experience authentic flavors and gain inspiration for your own cooking.
7	Pursue lifelong learning and personal growth by taking up courses to upskill yourself.	8	Snack on nuts and seeds for a satisfying crunch and healthy fats.
9	Share meals with loved ones and friends whenever possible to foster social connections.	10	Prepare larger quantities of Mediterranean staples like soups, grains, and legumes to use throughout the week.

11 Enhance and experiment flavor with Mediterranean herbs and spices rather than relying on excess salt. For more tips and recipes, refer to my bonus book on herbs and spices. See page 30.

12	Add legumes such as beans, lentils, and chickpeas in soups, salads, and stews for plant-based protein and fiber.	13	Use non-dairy milk alternatives like almond milk or coconut milk in your cooking and beverages.
14	Plan snacks ahead to avoid last-minute unhealthy choices.	15	Spend time outdoors to soak up sunlight and vitamin D.
16	Minimize processed and sugary foods like soda, candy, and packaged snacks.	17	Cultivate gratitude by reflecting on the flavors and enjoyment of each meal.
18	Walk up a hill or take the stairs whenever possible as it improves strength, balance and boosts heart rate.	19	Develop a pre-meal ritual such as setting the table beautifully or saying a few words of gratitude.

20	Get to know your neighbors. Make an extra portion of your favorite Mediterranean dish and share it with them.	21	Experiment with new unfamiliar ingredients and cooking techniques occasionally to keep meals exciting.

22 Embrace the Mediterranean philosophy of balance and moderation in all things, savoring indulgences like gelato or pastries on occasion while maintaining a foundation of nutrient-rich, whole foods in your diet.

23	Replace some of your regular tea or coffee with herbal teas like chamomile, mint, or sage for their health benefits.	24	Bake your own whole grain bread or try traditional Mediterranean bread recipes like pita or focaccia.
25	Limit red meat to once a week, opting for plant-based proteins or seafood on other days.	26	Take time to daydream. Visualize your dreams and hopes and what life would be like to have achieved them.
27	Visit a local farmer's market to support sustainable agriculture and find fresh Mediterranean ingredients.	28	Enhance your salads and marinades with balsamic, or apple cider vinegar to boost both flavor and health benefits.
29	Repurpose leftovers to create new meals or pack for lunches during the week.	30	Dine without distractions like screens or work to fully enjoy your meals.
31	Stay hydrated by carrying a reusable water bottle throughout the day.	32	Dedicate time weekly for meal prep and batch cooking for convenience.

33 Incorporate daily mindfulness practices such as meditation or deep breathing exercises to slow down and learn to live in the present, a key aspect of the Mediterranean approach to health.

34	Reserve dining out for special occasions and prioritize homemade meals.	35	Make effort to take regular breaks during the day to recharge and refresh.
36	Practice mindfulness while grocery shopping, focusing on selecting fresh, seasonal ingredients and avoiding processed foods.	37	Take time to appreciate the sensory experience of each meal, focusing on taste, texture, and aroma to enhance satisfaction and promote mindful consumption.
38	Enjoy post-meal walks to aid digestion and promote relaxation.	39	Indulge in treats occasionally, savoring each bite mindfully.
40	Create a Mediterranean-inspired podcast series exploring topics like nutrition, mindfulness, and sustainable living, featuring interviews with experts, chefs, and wellness influencers.	41	Engage in outdoor activities beyond traditional exercise, such as bird watching, or nature photography, to connect with nature and promote physical activity in a joyful, natural setting.

42 Focus on eating fruits and vegetables that are in season to ensure maximum freshness and nutrient content.

43 Take a vacation, go on a cruise or take a drive through the countryside to be away from your daily routine.

44 Explore Mediterranean-inspired dessert options for guilt-free enjoyment. Check our recipe section to discover delightful creations that capture the essence of the region's culinary traditions.

45 Write freely, without censoring or analyzing your thoughts, allowing for self-expression and reflection in your journal.

46 Make your own sauces such as tzatziki, pesto, or hummus to avoid preservatives and have control over the ingredients.

47 Start a book club focused on reading literature set.

48 Organize outdoor gatherings for picnics or barbecues with loved ones.

49 Attend Mediterranean-inspired cooking classes to expand culinary skills.

50 Establish boundaries and learn to say 'no' to balance work and leisure.

51 Create an outdoor relaxation space in your backyard or balcony, complete with cozy seating, soft lighting, and potted plants for a tranquil retreat.

52 Prioritize sleep hygiene (E.g. Bedtime Routine with no screen time one hour before turning down) for restorative rest each night.

53 Practice intermittent fasting, which is common in many Mediterranean cultures, to promote metabolic health.

54 Practice storytelling by gathering with friends and family to share tales and traditions passed down through generations.

55 Prioritize adequate hydration by incorporating herbal teas, citrus-infused water, and hydrating foods like cucumbers and melons into your daily routine, supporting overall health and well-being.

56 Carve out time for regular physical activity, whether it's a brisk walk, yoga, or cycling.

57 Create a vision board to visualize and set goals for your Mediterranean lifestyle.

58 Learn how to make skin care oil using essentials oils of Mediterranean herbs as they can have a calming and soothing effect.

59 Laugh a lot - watch a comedy show, read a comic or find the lighter side of life and share a funny story with a friend.

60 Develop a hobby related to Mediterranean culture, such as olive oil tasting or cheese making.

61 Join an interesting leisure group to establish newfound purpose and built new connections.

62 Start a daily journal to document your experiences and reflections on adopting the Mediterranean lifestyle.

63 Take conscious time to chill out and listen to your favorite music or explore genres like Flamenco or Italian opera.

64	Have a conversation with your younger or future you to forgive and accept the things in life. Practice self-compassion for emotional well-being.	65	Have at least 7 to 9 hours of sleep in the night 🌙 as it improves brain performance, maintain weight and may strengthen your heart.
66	Host a Mediterranean-inspired potluck dinner party with friends, where each guest brings a dish from a different Mediterranean country to create a diverse and delicious spread.		
67	Dedicate one day each month to a digital detox, where you unplug from technology.	68	Spend a day doing community work by offering service to people in need.
69	Do labyrinth walking, where you follow a winding path to quiet the mind and promote inner peace. 🌳	70	Make lunch your largest meal of the day, as is common in many Mediterranean cultures, to aid digestion and energy levels.
71	Engage in spontaneous acts of kindness, such as paying for a stranger's coffee or leaving uplifting notes in public spaces, to spread positivity and brighten someone's day.	72	Volunteer for environmental conservation projects focused on protecting coastal habitats, cleaning up beaches, and promoting sustainable practices to preserve the beauty.
73	Inject Mediterranean-inspired design elements into your home decor, such as whitewashed walls, natural textures, and vibrant blue accents reminiscent of the Mediterranean Sea.	74	Explore the coastline for opportunities to forage wild edibles like sea asparagus, samphire, or edible seaweeds, adding a sense of adventure and connection to the natural environment.
75	Explore alternative healing modalities like going for a massage, acupuncture, or energy healing to restore balance and harmony to mind, body, and spirit. 🕯️	76	Witness the beauty of sunrise or sunset to not only enjoy a serene moment but it also offers health benefits according to the Journal of Environmental Psychology.
77	Take a walk near the waters, live near the coastlines or add a water feature like a fountain in your home. Being near water has been linked to enhanced physical health according to a panel survey done in England.		
78	Cultivate a conscious effort to notice and appreciate the beauty and abundance in everyday life, from a sunrise to a kind gesture from a stranger.	79	Practice the art of letting go by decluttering your physical space, releasing attachments to material possessions, and simplifying your life.
80	Cultivate meaningful relationships with everyone you meet from your colleagues, community friends, neighbors for support and connection.	81	Join a local art class to explore Mediterranean art styles like mosaics or pottery that has a meditative element to them. 🎨

82	Adopt traditional methods like sun-drying tomatoes, curing olives, or preserving lemons to add authentic flavors to your meals.	**83**	Find ways to give love: Spend quality time with loved one by doing something that they love.
84	Explore the night sky through stargazing or learning about celestial bodies and constellations to foster a sense of awe and inquisitiveness.	**85**	Embrace the enriching companionship of pet ownership, fostering a bond filled with unconditional love, laughter, and endless cuddles.
86	Nurture your inner child by indulging in activities that spark wonder and imagination such as building sandcastles, and flying kites.	**87**	Adopt a role model whom you look up to achieve your life's goals with a positive mindset and resilience.

88 Foster connections through regular communication with loved ones. For example, setting aside time each evening to catch up with family members over dinner can provide an opportunity to share stories, discuss challenges, and offer support.

89	Explore new places, try new activities or hobbies, and embrace spontaneity in your daily life to cultivate a sense of adventure and wonder.	**90**	Develop resilience in life by reframing challenges as opportunities for growth, learning, and self-discovery, and finding strength in adversity.
91	Embrace the practice of forest bathing, immersing yourself in nature to reduce stress, boost immunity, and enhance overall well-being.	**92**	Build your own tribe. Create a circle of social support with likeminded friends to help your through crises and celebrate triumphs.
93	Give yourself a cheat day where you can treat and reward yourself. Choose a day when you have done an intense workout or have a special reason to celebrate.	**94**	Create a self-care routine, incorporating rituals like dry brushing, oil pulling, and herbal baths to nourish your body, mind, and spirit.
95	Reconnect with old friends or a childhood hobby that you love doing.	**96**	Change up your routine whether it's your jogging path, or journey to work etc.
97	Switch to natural cleaning products like vinegar, lemon, and olive oil commonly used in Mediterranean households.	**98**	Take time to celebrate special occasions, milestones, and cherish everyday moments with loved ones, friends, and colleagues.
99	Opt for whole grains like quinoa, farro, and brown rice instead of refined grains.	**100**	Practice kindness and compassion toward yourself and others.

These tips serve as a starting point to infuse the values of the Mediterranean lifestyle into your busy modern life, where you find time to connect with yourself and others and seek balance between work and life. With a bit of intentionality and creativity, you can enjoy the health, happiness, and vitality that come from embracing this enriching way of living.

CHAPTER 4

GETTING STARTED WITH THE MEDITERRANEAN DIET

Let each meal be a reminder of the joy in simplicity and the beauty of taking care of yourself, one flavorful step at a time.

EXPLORING COMMON QUESTIONS AND MYTHS

Now, let's unravel some common queries that may dance through your mind:

How should I compose my plate?

Visualize your plate as a masterpiece, with half dedicated to a vibrant array of fruits and vegetables, one-quarter to wholesome grains, and the remaining quarter to lean proteins such as fish or chicken. The visual guide on the right can help illuminate your culinary path with clarity and grace.

Are there any foods I should avoid, and what can I eat instead?

FOODS TO AVOID	FOODS TO EAT
Processed Food	Wholesome Snacks like Fruits,Nuts etc.
Refined ones	Whole wheat bread or brown rice
Processed Meats	Leaner protein such as chicken, fish, or beans
Sugary Treats	A dollop of honey on Greek yogurt

Following are some myths related to Mediterranean diet:

Myth 1: Adhering to a Mediterranean diet can be challenging.

If you're weary of diets, consider embracing this as a holistic way of life. The Mediterranean diet offers more than just a temporary solution—it fosters a healthy relationship with food, curbs overeating, and provides a sustainable approach for lifelong well-being with oneself and the community around you.

Myth 2: Weight-loss with the Mediterranean diet means bland meals and portion control.

Contrary to popular belief, this eating plan is anything but dull! Bursting with flavorful and diverse foods, it ensures balanced nutrition and wards off deprivation. Decades of research support its effectiveness in promoting natural and safe weight loss.

Myth 3: All fats are unhealthy.

In truth, the Mediterranean diet distinguishes between beneficial and harmful fats. Incorporating healthy fats such as avocado in moderation not only promotes radiant skin but also boosts energy levels and bolsters the immune system.

Myth 4: Grains lead to weight gain.

Many mistakenly believe that cutting carbs is the key to shedding pounds. However, including moderate portions of wholesome carbs like whole grains supports weight loss and sustains optimal health. A balanced diet comprising good carbs, protein, and healthy fats reduces the risk of obesity and related ailments.

TRANSITIONING TO THE DIET

As you embark on your journey to adopt the Mediterranean diet, it's essential to understand that it's not just about changing what's on your plate; it's about embracing a whole new approach to eating.

Step 1: Gradual Dietary Changes

Transitioning to the Mediterranean diet isn't about sudden, drastic shifts. It's a journey, and like any journey, it's best taken one step at a time. Start by incorporating Mediterranean-inspired meals into your weekly rotation. Choose one or two meals each week to adapt to fit the Mediterranean framework. For instance, swap a traditional meat-based pasta dish for a vegetable and bean-packed pasta primavera, or opt for a vibrant Greek salad with grilled chicken instead of your usual sandwich.

As you become more accustomed to the Mediterranean Diet's plate ratio for the different food groups and its cooking techniques and flavors, gradually increase the frequency of these meals until they become staples in your repertoire. This gradual approach allows your palate to adjust and ensures long-term success.

Step 2: Meal Planning Made Easy

Meal planning is your secret tool when it comes to mastering the Mediterranean diet. Begin by exploring the diverse array of recipes that align with Mediterranean principles. Look for dishes bursting with colorful fruits, vegetables, whole grains, legumes, nuts, seeds, and lean proteins. Once you've gathered your recipes, create a weekly meal plan that strikes a balance of flavors, textures, and nutrients.

This Cookbook provides you with ready-made weekly plans and shopping lists, taking the guesswork out of meal planning and ensuring you always have nutritious options at your fingertips. Consider batch cooking staple items like whole grains, legumes, and grilled vegetables to streamline meal prep throughout the week. And don't forget to embrace seasonal produce for the freshest flavors and maximum nutritional benefits.

With guidance and your dedication, transitioning to the Mediterranean diet will be a seamless and enjoyable experience. Let's embark on this journey together towards a healthier, more vibrant way of eating.

KEY INGREDIENTS AND PANTRY ESSENTIALS

Essential Items for Your Mediterranean-Inspired Pantry

Building a Mediterranean-inspired pantry is the first step to bringing the vibrant flavors of this renowned cuisine into your kitchen. Here are some key ingredients to keep on hand:

- **Olive Oil:** A cornerstone of the Mediterranean diet, extra virgin olive oil adds richness and depth to dishes.
- **Whole Grains:** Stock up on whole grains like bulgur, farro, quinoa, and brown rice for hearty and nutritious meal bases.
- **Legumes:** Beans, lentils, and chickpeas provide plant-based protein and fiber, essential for a balanced diet.
- **Herbs and Spices:** Infuse your meals with the aromatic flavors of the Mediterranean with herbs like basil, oregano, thyme, and spices such as cumin, coriander, and paprika.
- **Olives and Capers:** Add briny notes to your dishes with olives and capers, perfect for salads, pasta, and sauces.
- **Nuts and Seeds:** Almonds, walnuts, pine nuts, and sesame seeds lend crunch and nutrition to salads, grain dishes, and desserts.
- **Cheeses:** While moderation is key, cheeses like feta, Parmesan, and goat cheese add richness and tang to Mediterranean-inspired meals.
- **Fresh Produce:** Keep your kitchen stocked with a variety of fresh fruits and vegetables, choosing seasonal options whenever possible for the best flavor and nutrition.
- **Tomatoes:** Tomatoes are a versatile ingredient in Mediterranean cooking, whether diced, crushed, or in the form of tomato paste.

Tips for Stocking and Sourcing Ingredients

- **Quality Over Quantity:** Invest in high-quality ingredients, especially olive oil, as it forms the foundation of many Mediterranean dishes. Look for extra virgin olive oil with a robust flavor profile.
- **Explore Ethnic Markets:** Ethnic markets and specialty stores are treasure troves of Mediterranean ingredients, offering a wide selection of olives, cheeses, spices, and more.
- **Buy in Bulk:** Save money and reduce packaging waste by purchasing staples like grains, legumes, and nuts in bulk quantities.
- **Read Labels:** When selecting canned or packaged goods, read labels carefully to avoid added sugars, preservatives, and unnecessary additives.

By stocking your pantry with these essential ingredients and following our tips for sourcing and stocking, you'll be well-equipped to whip up delicious Mediterranean-inspired meals with ease.

SPECIFIC DIETARY PREFERENCES

In the recipes section, you will find recipes clearly marked for **vegetarians (V)** and those that are **gluten-free (GF)**, ensuring that our readers with specific dietary preferences or restrictions can easily identify suitable options.

PURPOSE OF THE COOKBOOK

My goal is to help rejuvenate your health with a delightful diet of delicious and nutrient-dense recipes. Whilst providing a comprehensive guide to healthy eating, I've added a roadmap to seamlessly adopt the Mediterranean lifestyle into its diet.

I hope this book and its bonus books become your trusty companion in the kitchen, guiding you towards healthier eating habits and a vibrant lifestyle.

Enjoy every bite, cherish every moment, and remember - good health is the ultimate recipe for happiness.

BONUS GUIDEBOOKS

BONUS #1 – SPICE & HERB ESSENTIALS: A COMPREHENSIVE GUIDE TO ENHANCING YOUR MEDITERRANEAN DIET WITH FLAVORFUL INGREDIENTS

Discover the wonderful world of Mediterranean seasonings by learning the fundamentals of flavor profiles and health benefits of its primary herbs and spices. Learn simple tips to add parsley, basil, paprika and more to your cooking while boosting taste and nutrition effortlessly.

BONUS #2 – LAVISH DISHES FOR THE WEEKENDS & FAMILIAL GATHERINGS: 25 CLASSIC MEDITERRANEAN RECIPES TO EAT, COOK & PARTAKE TOGETHER

Turn ordinary gatherings into extraordinary feasts with our collection of recipes to enhance the joy of shared meals with loved ones and friends. From savory main courses to decadent desserts, these recipes are crafted to create memorable moments and bring people together.

BONUS #3 – HEALTHY MEDITERRANEAN SMOOTHIES RECIPE BOOK

Indulge in the revitalizing flavors of Mediterranean-inspired smoothies. Each smoothie recipe has been carefully crafted to include a balance of nutrient-dense ingredients from heart-healthy fats to fiber-rich fruits and vegetables that support overall health.

TO GET INSTANT ACCESS GO TO:

https://heartbookspress.com/sciencebackedmediterranean-free-bonuses

You can also scan the QR Code below with your cell phone camera and tap on the link that pops up if you find that easier.

CHAPTER 5

DIPS, SAUCES AND CONDIMENTS

Indulge in the rich and diverse flavors of the Mediterranean with a tantalizing array of dips, sauces, and condiments that promise to elevate every meal.

Let the delightful flavors of the Mediterranean dance on your palate as each dip, sauces and condiments injects a spark of fun and vitality.

TIPS:

· Select the freshest and highest-quality ingredients to ensure your dips, sauces, and condiments are packed with vibrant flavors.

· Prepare your recipes in advance and store them in the fridge for up to a week to let the flavors meld and intensify.

· Serve with options like pita bread, crisp vegetables, or gourmet crackers for a delicious and versatile snack or appetizer, or for healthy snacking—keep a batch in the fridge to quickly satisfy cravings with chopped carrots, celery or any vegetable sticks.

Greek Olive Essence

V | GF

PREP TIME 10 MIN **COOK TIME** 0 MIN **SERVINGS** 8

INGREDIENTS:

- 1 cup pitted Kalamata olives
- 2 cloves garlic, minced
- 1 tbsp fresh lemon juice
- 2 tbsp extra virgin olive oil
- 1 tsp dried oregano
- Salt and pepper to taste

INSTRUCTIONS:

1 In a food processor, combine the pitted Kalamata olives and minced garlic.
2 Pulse until the olives and garlic are finely chopped. Add the fresh lemon juice, extra virgin olive oil, and dried oregano to the food processor.
3 Continue to pulse until the mixture forms a smooth paste.
4 Taste the mixture and season with salt and pepper according to taste.
5 Transfer the essence to a serving dish like salads, grilled vegetables or fish.

NUTRITIONAL FACTS (PER SERVING): *Calories: 80, Carbohydrates: 2g, Protein: 0g, Fat: 8g, Fiber: 1g*

FUN FACTS AND HEALTH BENEFIT:

Greek Olive Essence is often used in Mediterranean dishes for its rich, fruity flavor. In ancient Greece, olive oil was called "liquid gold" by Homer in ancient Greece.

It's packed with antioxidants and healthy fats that promote heart health and reduce inflammation.

Provence Herb Infusion

V | GF

PREP TIME 5 MIN **COOK TIME** 5 MIN **SERVINGS** 4

INGREDIENTS:

- 2 cups water
- 2 sprigs fresh rosemary
- 4 sprigs fresh thyme
- 1 bay leaf
- 1 tsp dried lavender buds (optional)

INSTRUCTIONS:

1 Boil 2 cups of water in a saucepan.
2 Rinse and dry 2 sprigs each of rosemary and thyme.
3 Add the herbs and 1 bay leaf to the boiling water.
4 Optional: Add 1 tsp of dried lavender buds.
5 Simmer for 3-4 minutes.
6 Remove from heat and let it cool slightly.
7 Strain the infusion to remove herbs.
8 Discard the herbs and transfer the infusion to a serving pitcher. Use it over roasted meats, soups, grilled fish, bread etc.

NUTRITIONAL FACTS (PER SERVING): *Calories:10, Carbohydrates: 2g, Protein: 1g, Fat: 0g, Fiber: 0g*

FUN FACTS AND HEALTH BENEFIT:

Provence Herb Infusion enhances dishes with the aromatic blend. Herbs were traditionally used in French cooking to mask the smell of aging meats.

They contain antioxidants that help improve digestion and reduce inflammation.

Aegean Herb Drizzle V | GF

PREP TIME 10 MIN **COOK TIME** 0 MIN **SERVINGS** 6

INGREDIENTS:

- 1/2 cup extra virgin olive oil
- 2 tbsp fresh lemon juice
- 2 cloves garlic, minced
- 1 tsp coconut cream
- 1 tbsp chopped parsley
- 1 tsp dried oregano
- 1/2 tsp dried thyme
- Salt and pepper to taste

INSTRUCTIONS:

1. Whisk olive oil and lemon juice in a bowl.
2. Add garlic, parsley, oregano, thyme.
3. Season with salt and pepper.
4. Whisk until herbs blend.
5. Taste and adjust seasoning. Drizzle with coconut cream.
6. Transfer to container.
7. Drizzle on cooked meats, veggies, or used as a marinade.

NUTRITIONAL FACTS (PER SERVING): *Calories: 50, Carbohydrates: 1g, Protein: 0g, Fat: 5g, Fiber: 0g*

FUN FACTS AND HEALTH BENEFIT:

Aegean Herb Drizzle is known for its vibrant taste. Oregano, a key ingredient, was believed to bring good luck and health in ancient Greece.

This drizzle is rich in antioxidants, promoting overall health and boosting the immune system.

Mediterranean Spice Blend V | GF

PREP TIME 5 MIN **COOK TIME** 0 MIN **SERVINGS** 12

INGREDIENTS:

- 2 tbsp dried oregano
- 2 tbsp dried basil
- 1 tbsp dried thyme
- 1 tbsp dried rosemary
- 1 tbsp garlic powder
- 1 tbsp onion powder
- 1 tbsp paprika
- 1 tsp ground black pepper
- 1 tsp kosher salt

INSTRUCTIONS:

1. Mix all dried herbs and spices.
2. Stir until well blended.
3. Transfer to airtight container.
4. Store in cool, dry place.
5. Sprinkle on grilled vegetables, seafood, or roasted chicken etc.

NUTRITIONAL FACTS (PER SERVING): *Calories: 5, Carbohydrates: 1g, Protein: 0g, Fat: 0g, Fiber: 0g*

FUN FACTS AND HEALTH BENEFIT:

This Mediterranean blend offers a symphony of flavors. The ancient Greeks and Romans believed that basil symbolized love and fertility.

This blend not only adds depth to dishes but also boasts antimicrobial properties, supporting digestive health.

Tuscan Sun Dip

V

PREP TIME 15 MIN   **COOK TIME** 0 MIN   **SERVINGS** 8

INGREDIENTS:

- 2 cup sun-dried tomatoes (packed in oil), drained
- 1/2 cup grated Parmesan cheese
- 1/4 cup chopped fresh basil
- 2 cloves garlic, minced
- 1/4 cup extra virgin olive oil
- Salt and pepper to taste

INSTRUCTIONS:

1 Blend sun-dried tomatoes, Parmesan, basil, garlic.
2 Pulse until thick paste forms.
3 Gradually add olive oil while blending.
4 Season with salt, pepper.
5 Transfer to serving bowl.
6 Serve with crackers, breadsticks, or veggies.

NUTRITIONAL FACTS (PER SERVING): *Calories: 60, Carbohydrates: 2g, Protein: 1g, Fat: 6g, Fiber: 0g*

FUN FACTS AND HEALTH BENEFIT:

The Tuscan Sun Dip captures the essence of Italy. Sun-dried tomatoes were originally dried under the Italian sun to preserve them for the winter months.

This dip is not only bursting with flavor but also rich in lycopene, promoting skin health.

Sicilian Citrus Zest

V | GF

PREP TIME 10 MIN   **COOK TIME** 5 MIN   **SERVINGS** 6

INGREDIENTS:

- Zest of 2 lemons
- Zest of 2 oranges
- Zest of 1 lime
- 2 tbsp fresh lemon juice
- 2 tbsp orange juice
- 1 tbsp fresh lime juice
- 1 tsp honey
- Pinch of salt

INSTRUCTIONS:

1 Combine lemon, orange, and lime zest in a bowl.
2 Add lemon, orange, and lime juice, plus honey.
3 Season with a pinch of salt.
4 Stir until well combined.
5 Adjust sweetness or acidity to taste.
6 Transfer to a container.
7 Use as a topping on baked goods, marinade, or in salads or dressings.

NUTRITIONAL FACTS (PER SERVING): *Calories: 10, Carbohydrates: 3g, Protein: 0g, Fat: 0g, Fiber: 0g*

FUN FACTS AND HEALTH BENEFIT:

Citrus fruits have been cultivated in Sicily, Southern Italy, since ancient times, with records dating back to the 10th century.

This zest is not only flavorful but also packed with vitamin C, boosting immunity.

CHAPTER 6

BREAKFASTS

Capture the essence of the Mediterranean sunrise with each breakfast bite, as these recipes infuse your mornings with a burst of flavor and a touch of Mediterranean magic, promising to transform your day from the very first taste.

Let the vibrant hues of a Mediterranean breakfast awaken your senses, inspiring you to nourish each day with zest and thankfulness.

TIPS:

· Incorporate fresh fruits, nuts, and seeds into your breakfast for added nutrition and flavor.

· Experiment with different herbs and spices to add depth to your breakfast dishes.

· Make ahead and refrigerate or freeze for a quick and easy breakfast on-the-go.

· Don't be afraid to get creative with leftovers — yesterday's dinner can become today's breakfast!

Labneh

V | GF

PREP TIME 5 MIN **COOK TIME** 0 MIN **SERVINGS** 16

INGREDIENTS:

· 2 cups plain yogurt
· 1/2 tsp salt
· Olive oil (optional, for serving)
· Fresh herbs (such as mint or parsley) (optional, for serving)
· Za'atar spice blend (optional, for serving)

INSTRUCTIONS:

1 Mix plain yogurt and salt in bowl.
2 Stir until salt is fully mixed.
3 Line sieve with cheesecloth over bowl.
4 Pour yogurt mixture into sieve.
5 Tie cheesecloth edges to form bundle.
6 Hang bundle over bowl in fridge for 12-24 hours.
7 Once strained, transfer labneh to serving bowl.
8 Drizzle with olive oil; sprinkle with herbs and za'atar if desired.
9 Serve labneh with bread, crackers, or veggies.

NUTRITIONAL FACTS (PER SERVING): *Calories: 60, Carbohydrates: 2g, Protein: 2g, Fat: 5g, Fiber: 0g*

FUN FACTS AND HEALTH BENEFIT:

Labneh, a creamy Mediterranean yogurt cheese, is a versatile delight. Its origins trace back to ancient times, with references found in historical texts.

Labneh is not only delicious but also rich in probiotics, supporting gut health and digestion.

Shakshuka

V | GF

PREP TIME 10 MIN **COOK TIME** 20 MIN **SERVINGS** 2

INGREDIENTS:

· 2 tbsp olive oil
· 1 onion, chopped
· 2 cloves garlic, minced
· 1 red bell pepper, diced
· 1 can (14 oz) diced tomatoes
· 1 tsp cumin
· 1 tsp paprika
· 1/2 tsp chili powder (adjust to taste)
· Salt and pepper to taste
· 4 eggs
· Fresh parsley or cilantro, chopped (for garnish)

INSTRUCTIONS:

1 Heat olive oil in skillet.
2 Sauté onions until translucent (3-4 mins).
3 Add garlic, bell pepper; cook until soft (2-3 mins).
4 Pour in diced tomatoes, spices; including cumin and paprika, simmer 10-15 mins.
5 Make wells in sauce; crack eggs into wells.
6 Cover and cook eggs for 5-7 mins.
7 Remove from heat. Garnish with parsley.
8 Serve immediately with bread.

NUTRITIONAL FACTS (PER SERVING): *Calories: 300, Carbohydrates: 15g, Protein: 15g, Fat: 20g, Fiber: 5g*

FUN FACTS AND HEALTH BENEFIT:

Shakshuka, a brunch favorite, translates to "all mixed up", reflecting its diverse blend of flavors.

Nutritionally, it's packed with protein from eggs and vitamins from tomatoes, supporting overall health and energy levels.

Frittata

PREP TIME 10 MIN   **COOK TIME** 20 MIN   **SERVINGS** 4

INGREDIENTS:

- 6 eggs
- 1/4 cup milk/soy milk
- Salt and pepper to taste
- 1 tbsp olive oil
- 1 small onion, chopped
- 1 bell pepper, diced
- 1 cup baby spinach, chopped
- 1/2 cup cherry tomatoes, halved
- 1/2 cup shredded cheese
- Fresh herbs (such as parsley, basil, or chives), chopped

INSTRUCTIONS:

1 Preheat oven to 350°F (175°C).
2 Whisk eggs, milk, salt, and pepper in a bowl.
3 Heat olive oil in oven-safe skillet.
4 Sauté onion and bell pepper until soft (3-4 min).
5 Add spinach, tomatoes; cook until spinach wilts.
6 Pour egg mixture over veggies. And sprinkle cheese on top. Cook on stovetop until edges set (3-4 mins). Bake in oven for 10-12 mins until set. Let cool briefly before slicing.
7 Garnish with fresh herbs.

NUTRITIONAL FACTS (PER SERVING): *Calories: 250, Carbohydrates: 10g, Protein: 20g, Fat: 15g, Fiber: 2g*

FUN FACTS AND HEALTH BENEFIT:

The frittata, with its Italian roots, is a versatile egg dish. Perfect for using up leftovers or spare pantry ingredients.

This dish offers a balanced mix of protein, vitamins, and minerals, promoting muscle strength and overall well-being.

Tabbouleh

PREP TIME 15 MIN   **COOK TIME** 0 MIN   **SERVINGS** 4

INGREDIENTS:

- 1 cup bulgur wheat
- 2 cups water
- 2 cups fresh parsley, finely chopped
- 1 cup cherry tomatoes, diced
- 1/2 cup cucumber, diced
- 1/4 cup red onion, finely chopped
- 1/4 cup fresh mint leaves, finely chopped
- 2 tbsp olive oil
- 2 tbsp lemon juice
- Salt and pepper to taste

INSTRUCTIONS:

1 Combine bulgur wheat and boiling water in medium bowl; let sit 10 mins.
2 Fluff bulgur with fork; transfer to large mixing bowl.
3 Add parsley, tomatoes, cucumber, red onion, mint to bowl.
4 Drizzle olive oil, lemon juice over salad.
5 Season with salt, pepper to taste.
6 Toss until well combined. Serve immediately.

NUTRITIONAL FACTS (PER SERVING): *Calories: 150, Carbohydrates: 25g, Protein: 5g, Fat: 5g, Fiber: 5g*

FUN FACTS AND HEALTH BENEFIT:

Tabbouleh, is often considered the "queen of salads", admired for its vibrant colors and fresh flavors.

It is a nutrient-rich powerhouse, offering a boost of fiber, vitamins, and antioxidants, supporting digestive health.

Mediterranean Chickpea Pancakes

V | GF

PREP TIME 10 MIN **COOK TIME** 15 MIN **SERVINGS** 4

INGREDIENTS:

- 1 cup chickpea flour
- 1 cup water
- 2 tbsp olive oil
- 1 tsp salt
- 1/2 tsp ground cumin
- 1/2 tsp paprika
- Fresh herbs for garnish (optional)

INSTRUCTIONS:

1 In a mixing bowl, whisk together chickpea flour, water, olive oil, salt, cumin, and paprika until smooth.
2 Let the batter rest for 10 minutes.
3 Heat a non-stick skillet over medium heat and brush with olive oil.
4 Pour a ladleful of batter into the skillet, spreading it evenly into a thin pancake.
5. Cook for 2-3 minutes on each side until golden brown and crispy.
6 Repeat with the remaining batter.
7 Garnish with fresh herbs if desired and serve.

NUTRITIONAL FACTS (PER SERVING): *Calories: 170, Carbohydrates: 19g, Protein: 7g, Fat: 8g, Fiber: 4g*

FUN FACTS AND HEALTH BENEFIT:

Chickpea Pancakes Socca originated in Nice, France, but it is popular across the Mediterranean region.

Socca, made with chickpea flour, offers a gluten-free, protein and fiber-rich promoting digestive health and sustained energy with its abundance of vitamins and minerals.

Omelette with Spinach and Feta

V | GF

PREP TIME 5 MIN **COOK TIME** 5 MIN **SERVINGS** 1

INGREDIENTS:

- 2 eggs
- 1/2 cup fresh spinach leaves, chopped
- 1/4 cup crumbled feta cheese
- Salt and pepper to taste
- 1 tbsp olive oil

INSTRUCTIONS:

1 Beat eggs in mixing bowl.
2 Add spinach, feta, salt, pepper; stir.
3 Heat olive oil in skillet (medium heat).
4 Pour egg mixture into skillet; spread evenly.
5 Cook for 2-3 mins until edges set.
6 Lift edges with spatula to let uncooked eggs flow.
7 Continue cooking until set but moist on top
8 Fold omelette in half. Slide onto plate; serve hot.

NUTRITIONAL FACTS (PER SERVING): *Calories: 250, Carbohydrates: 3g, Protein: 18g, Fat: 18g, Fiber: 1g*

FUN FACTS AND HEALTH BENEFIT:

Omelettes date back to ancient time, where they were enjoyed by royalty.

This delectable dish offers a protein-packed start to the day, supporting muscle repair and providing essential vitamins and minerals for overall health and well-being.

Mediterranean Breakfast Sandwich

V

PREP TIME 5 MIN **COOK TIME** 5 MIN **SERVINGS** 1

INGREDIENTS:

- 2 slices whole grain bread
- 1 egg
- 1/4 cup baby spinach leaves
- 2 slices tomato
- 2 slices cucumber
- 1 slice feta cheese
- 1 tbsp hummus
- Salt and pepper to taste
- Olive oil or cooking spray for cooking

INSTRUCTIONS:

1 Heat skillet over medium heat, coat with olive oil.
2 Crack egg into skillet; cook to desired doneness.
3. Toast bread slices until golden brown.
4. Spread hummus on one slice of bread.
5 Layer spinach, tomato, cucumber, feta on hummus. Place cooked egg on veggies.
6 Season with salt, pepper.
7 Top with second slice of bread.
8 Slice diagonally; serve immediately.

NUTRITIONAL FACTS (PER SERVING): *Calories: 350, Carbohydrates: 30g, Protein: 15g, Fat: 25g, Fiber: 5g*

FUN FACTS AND HEALTH BENEFIT:

This Mediterranean Sandwich brings a twist to your morning routine, making your breakfast feel like a gourmet experience from the sunny shores of Greece.

It provides a balanced meal, rich in protein, fiber, and healthy fats, promoting sustained energy and satiety throughout the morning

Greek Scrambled Eggs (Strapatsada)

V | GF

PREP TIME 10 MIN **COOK TIME** 10 MIN **SERVINGS** 2

INGREDIENTS:

- 4 large eggs
- 2 ripe tomatoes, grated or finely chopped
- 50g feta cheese, crumbled
- 2 tbsp olive oil
- Salt and pepper to taste
- Fresh oregano or basil for garnish (optional)

INSTRUCTIONS:

1 Heat olive oil in a skillet over medium heat.
2 Add grated tomatoes and cook until softened.
3 In a bowl, beat the eggs and pour into the skillet.
4 Stir gently until the eggs start to set.
5 Add crumbled feta cheese and continue cooking until eggs are fully cooked but still moist.
6 Season with salt and pepper, garnish with fresh herbs if desired, and serve hot.

NUTRITIONAL FACTS (PER SERVING): *Calories: 240, Carbohydrates: 5g, Protein: 15g, Fat: 18g, Fiber: 1g*

FUN FACTS AND HEALTH BENEFIT:

Strapatsada is a traditional Greek dish often enjoyed for breakfast or as a light lunch. Its simple yet flavorful ingredients make it a staple in Mediterranean cuisine

This dish is a protein-rich blend of eggs and feta cheese, complemented by antioxidant-packed tomatoes and heart-healthy olive oil.

Avocado Toast _V

PREP TIME 5 MIN **COOK TIME** 5 MIN **SERVINGS** 1

INGREDIENTS:

- *1 ripe avocado*
- *2 slices whole grain bread, toasted*
- *Salt and pepper to taste*
- *Optional toppings: cherry tomatoes, red pepper flakes, feta cheese, poached egg, smoked salmon, arugula, balsamic glaze*

INSTRUCTIONS:

1 Cut avocado in half, remove pit, and scoop flesh into bowl.

2 Mash avocado with fork to desired consistency.

3 Season with salt and pepper; stir.

4 Spread avocado on toasted bread.

5 Add toppings like tomatoes, red pepper flakes, feta, or poached egg.

6 Serve immediately while bread is warm.

NUTRITIONAL FACTS (PER SERVING): *Calories: 250, Carbohydrates: 25g, Protein: 5g, Fat: 15g, Fiber: 7g*

FUN FACTS AND HEALTH BENEFIT:

Avocado's consumption has historical roots in Mesoamerican cultures like the Aztecs, who revered it as a symbol of fertility and love.

This Mediterranean inspired dish offers a wealth of healthy fats, fiber, and vitamins, fostering heart health and radiant skin.

Spanish Potato Omelette _{V | GF}

PREP TIME 10 MIN **COOK TIME** 20 MIN **SERVINGS** 4

INGREDIENTS:

- *4 medium potatoes, peeled and thinly sliced*
- *1 onion, thinly sliced*
- *4 eggs*
- *Salt and pepper to taste*
- *Olive oil for frying*

INSTRUCTIONS:

1 Cook potatoes and onions in olive oil until tender.

2 Beat eggs, season, and mix with cooked potatoes and onions.

3 Cook egg mixture in skillet until set.

4 Flip and cook the other side until golden.

5 Serve warm or at room temperature.

NUTRITIONAL FACTS (PER SERVING): *Calories: 300, Carbohydrates: 25g, Protein: 8g, Fat: 18g, Fiber: 3g*

FUN FACTS AND HEALTH BENEFIT:

Despite its name, the Spanish Potato Omelette, or "Tortilla Española," is not an omelette in the traditional sense but rather a thick, hearty potato cake.

This classic Spanish dish offers a satisfying mix of carbohydrates, protein, and nutrients.

Mediterranean Diet Oatmeal

V | GF

PREP TIME 2 MIN **COOK TIME** 5 MIN **SERVINGS** 2

INGREDIENTS:

- 1 cup old-fashioned oats
- 2 cups water or milk (or a combination)
- 1 tbsp honey or maple syrup
- 1/4 tsp ground cinnamon
- 1/2 cup mixed fresh berries
- 2 tbsp chopped nuts
- Greek yogurt for serving

INSTRUCTIONS:

1 Cook oats in water or milk until creamy.
2 Add honey or maple syrup and cinnamon.
3 Serve topped with berries, nuts and Greek yogurt.
4 Optionally, drizzle with more honey or syrup. Enjoy!

NUTRITIONAL FACTS (PER SERVING): *Calories: 300, Carbohydrates: 45g, Protein: 8g, Fat: 10g, Fiber: 7g*

FUN FACTS AND HEALTH BENEFIT:

Mediterranean Diet Oatmeal offers a nutritious twist on a breakfast classic. It emphasizes whole grains like oats for sustained energy and fiber.

This oatmeal also provides essential nutrients, promoting heart health and overall well-being.

Bruschetta with Tomato and Basil

V

PREP TIME 10 MIN **COOK TIME** 10 MIN **SERVINGS** 4

INGREDIENTS:

- 1 baguette, sliced into 1/2-inch thick slices
- 2 ripe tomatoes, diced
- 2 cloves garlic, minced
- 1/4 cup fresh basil leaves, chopped
- 2 tbsp extra virgin olive oil
- 1 tbsp balsamic vinegar
- Salt and pepper to taste

INSTRUCTIONS:

1 Preheat grill to medium heat.
2 Grill baguette slices 2-3 mins per side.
3 Mix tomatoes, garlic, basil, olive oil, balsamic vinegar in a bowl.
4 Season with salt, pepper; toss.
5 Spoon mixture over grilled bread.
6 Serve immediately.

NUTRITIONAL FACTS (PER SERVING): *Calories: 150, Carbohydrates: 15g, Protein: 4g, Fat: 2g, Fiber: 8*

FUN FACTS AND HEALTH BENEFIT:

Originating from central Italy, bruschetta was originally a way to use up stale bread.

This dish not only delights the taste buds but also offers a burst of antioxidants from fresh tomatoes and herbs, supporting immune health and vitality.

APPETIZERS

Explore the vibrant flavors of the Mediterranean with a tantalizing array of small plates, fresh ingredients and bold flavor combinations to kick off any gathering or snack time in style.

Dabble your way through the vibrant Mediterranean palette, where each appetizer beckons you to relish the present and craft lasting memories.

TIPS:

- Balance flavors by offering a variety of tastes, including sweet, savory, tangy, and spicy options to please every palate.

- Consider dietary restrictions and allergies when planning your appetizers, offering a selection of vegetarian, gluten-free, and dairy-free options to accommodate all guests.

- Elevate presentation by playing with plating techniques, garnishes, and serving vessels, create visually appealing dishes that are as beautiful as they are delicious.

- Encourage guest engagement by using interactive elements in your appetizers, such as DIY assembly stations, fostering a sense of fun and participation among your guests.

33

Greek Dolmades V | GF

PREP TIME 15 MIN **COOK TIME** 25 MIN **SERVINGS** 4

INGREDIENTS:

- 1 jar grape leaves, drained and rinsed
- 1 cup uncooked rice
- 1/2 cup chopped fresh dill
- 1/4 cup pine nuts, toasted
- 1/4 cup raisins, chopped
- 1 onion, finely chopped
- 2 cloves garlic, minced
- 2 tbsp olive oil
- Juice of 1 lemon
- Salt and pepper to taste
- Greek yogurt

INSTRUCTIONS:

1. Sauté onion and garlic in olive oil.
2. Mix with uncooked rice, dill, pine nuts, raisins, lemon juice, olive oil, salt, and pepper.
3. Place mixture on grape leaves, fold, and roll tightly.
4. Arrange in pot, cover with water, weigh down, and simmer for 20-25 minutes.
5. Serve warm or at room temperature with Greek yogurt.

NUTRITIONAL FACTS (PER SERVING): *Calories: 250, Carbohydrates: 35g, Protein: 5g, Fat: 10g, Fiber: 3g*

FUN FACTS AND HEALTH BENEFIT:

The name 'dolma' has been borrowed by the Greeks from the Turks, but the dish itself dates back to ancient times and was mentioned by the famous philosopher Aristotle.

These tasty bites are not only flavorful but also rich in vitamins, minerals, and antioxidants, promoting overall health and well-being.

Turkish Sigara Böreği V

PREP TIME 15 MIN **COOK TIME** 10 MIN **SERVINGS** 8

INGREDIENTS:

- 8 sheets phyllo pastry
- 200g feta cheese, crumbled
- 100g mozzarella cheese, shredded
- 1/4 cup parsley, finely chopped
- 1 egg, beaten
- Olive oil for frying
- Sesame seeds for garnish (optional)

INSTRUCTIONS:

1. Mix feta, mozzarella, and parsley.
2. Spread mixture on phyllo sheets, roll tightly.
3. Seal with beaten egg.
4. Fry until golden and crispy.
5. Garnish with sesame seeds and serve hot.

NUTRITIONAL FACTS (PER SERVING): *Calories: 160, Carbohydrates: 10g, Protein: 7g, Fat: 10g, Fiber: 1g*

FUN FACTS AND HEALTH BENEFIT:

Turkish Sigara Böreği, crispy pastry rolls filled with cheese or meat, are a popular snack. These pastries get their name because they resemble cigars in shape.

They are a source of protein and calcium, especially when filled with cheese, supporting bone health and muscle function.

Caprese Skewers

V | GF

PREP TIME 15 MIN **COOK TIME** 0 MIN **SERVINGS** 4

INGREDIENTS:

- 12 cherry tomatoes
- 12 small fresh mozzarella balls
- 12 fresh basil leaves
- 2 tbsp balsamic glaze
- Salt and pepper to taste
- 12 small skewers

INSTRUCTIONS:

1. Wash and dry tomatoes and basil.
2. Skewer tomato, mozzarella, and basil.
3. Arrange on platter.
4. Drizzle with balsamic glaze.
5. Season with salt and pepper.
6. Serve and enjoy!

NUTRITIONAL FACTS (PER SERVING-3 SKEWERS):

Calories:120, Carbohydrates: 6g, Protein: 7g, Fat: 8g, Fiber: 2g

FUN FACTS AND HEALTH BENEFIT:

Caprese Skewers, a bite-sized version of the classic Italian dish. It is named after the island of Capri, where it was created to resemble the colors of the Italian flag.

These skewers are packed with vitamins, antioxidants, and calcium, supporting bone health and immune function.

Garlic Shrimp

GF

PREP TIME 15-20 MIN **COOK TIME** 4-6 MIN **SERVINGS** 2

INGREDIENTS:

- 1 lb shrimp, peeled and deveined
- 4 cloves garlic, minced
- 2 tbsp olive oil
- 2 tbsp lemon juice
- Salt and pepper to taste
- Fresh parsley for garnish

INSTRUCTIONS:

1. Combine shrimp, garlic, olive oil, lemon juice, salt, and pepper. Marinate for 15-20 minutes.
2. Heat skillet over medium-high heat. Cook shrimp until pink and opaque, about 2-3 minutes per side.
3. Transfer to plate, garnish with parsley, and serve.

NUTRITIONAL FACTS (PER SERVING): *Calories: 180, Carbohydrates: 2g, Protein: 24g, Fat: 9g, Fiber: 0g*

FUN FACTS AND HEALTH BENEFIT:

Garlic Shrimp, a popular Spanish dish. Garlic has been used for centuries for its medicinal properties including boosting immunity and reducing blood pressure.

This dish is a source of protein and healthy fats, supporting muscle repair and brain function.

Greek Tzatziki with Pita Bread

V

PREP TIME 10 MIN **COOK TIME** 0 MIN **SERVINGS** 4

INGREDIENTS:

- 1 cup Greek yogurt
- 1 cucumber, grated and squeezed to remove excess moisture
- 2 cloves garlic, minced
- 1 tbsp extra virgin olive oil
- 1 tbsp lemon juice
- 1 tbsp chopped fresh dill
- Salt and pepper to taste
- Pita bread / Focaccia for serving

INSTRUCTIONS:

1 Grate and drain cucumber.
2 Mix with yogurt, garlic, olive oil, lemon juice, and dill.
3 Season to taste.
4 Chill if desired.
5 Serve with pita bread or Focaccia.

NUTRITIONAL FACTS (PER SERVING): *Calories: 150, Carbohydrates: 10g, Protein: 5g, Fat: 10g, Fiber: 0*

FUN FACTS AND HEALTH BENEFIT:

Tzatziki has ancient roots, with variations found in Greek, Turkish, and across several Middle Eastern cuisines.

This refreshing dip offers probiotics from the yogurt, promoting gut health and digestion.

Espinacas con garbanzos

V | GF

PREP TIME 10 MIN **COOK TIME** 15 MIN **SERVINGS** 2

INGREDIENTS:

- 2 tbsp olive oil
- 1 onion, chopped
- 2 cloves garlic, minced
- 1 tsp smoked paprika
- 1/2 tsp cumin
- 1 can (15 oz) chickpeas, drained and rinsed
- 1 lb spinach, washed and chopped
- Lemon wedges for serving

INSTRUCTIONS:

1 Heat olive oil in a large skillet over medium heat. Add chopped onion and minced garlic. Cook until softened.
2 Stir in smoked paprika and cumin. Add chickpeas to the skillet and cook for 2-3 minutes.
3 Gradually add chopped spinach to the skillet, allowing it to wilt. Cook until the spinach is tender and wilted. Season with salt and pepper.
4 Serve hot with lemon wedges on the side.

NUTRITIONAL FACTS (PER SERVING): *Calories: 180, Carbohydrates: 18g, Protein: 8g, Fat: 9g, Fiber: 6g*

FUN FACTS AND HEALTH BENEFIT:

Spinach with chickpeas, also known as "espinacas con garbanzos," has ancient origins, dating back to Moorish Spain.

This hearty dish is rich in protein, fiber, and essential nutrients, offering a satisfying and wholesome meal.

Mediterranean Grilled Vegetables

V | GF

PREP TIME 10 MIN **COOK TIME** 10 MIN **SERVINGS** 4

INGREDIENTS:

- 2 zucchinis, sliced
- 1 eggplant, sliced
- 1 red bell pepper, sliced
- 1 yellow bell pepper, sliced
- 1 red onion, sliced
- 2 tbsp olive oil
- 2 cloves garlic, minced
- 1 tsp dried oregano
- Salt and pepper to taste

INSTRUCTIONS:

1 Preheat grill to medium-high.
2 Toss zucchini, eggplant, bell peppers, and onion with oil, garlic, oregano, salt, and pepper.
3 Grill veggies for 5 mins per side until tender and charred.
4 Transfer to a platter.
5 Serve hot or at room temp as a side or in a Mediterranean meal.

NUTRITIONAL FACTS (PER SERVING): *Calories: 80, Carbohydrates: 10g, Protein: 2g, Fat: 5g, Fiber: 4g*

FUN FACTS AND HEALTH BENEFIT:

Grilling vegetables has been a traditional cooking method in the Mediterranean for centuries, enhancing their natural flavors.

This dish is packed with vitamins, minerals, and antioxidants, supporting overall health and vitality.

Quick Zucchini Stuffed Boats

V | GF

PREP TIME 10 MIN **COOK TIME** 20 MIN **SERVINGS** 8

INGREDIENTS:

- 4 medium zucchinis
- 1 cup cooked quinoa
- 1 cup cherry tomatoes, halved
- 1/2 cup crumbled feta cheese
- 1/4 cup chopped fresh basil
- 2 tbsp olive oil
- 2 cloves garlic, minced
- Grated Parmesan cheese for topping

INSTRUCTIONS:

1 Preheat oven to 375°F.
2 Halve zucchinis lengthwise and hollow them out.
3 In a bowl, mix quinoa, cherry tomatoes, feta cheese, basil, olive oil, garlic, salt, and pepper.
4 Fill zucchini halves with the mixture.
5 Bake for 20 minutes or until zucchinis are tender.
6 Sprinkle with grated Parmesan cheese and serve.

NUTRITIONAL FACTS (PER SERVING): *Calories: 210, Carbohydrates: 20g, Protein: 9g, Fat: 11g, Fiber: 4g*

FUN FACTS AND HEALTH BENEFIT:

These stuffed boats showcase the ingenuity of Mediterranean cuisine. Did you know that zucchinis are technically fruits, botanically classified as berries?

Zucchinis are low in calories and rich in essential nutrients like vitamins C and K, potassium, and antioxidants.

Pumpkin and Walnut

V | GF

PREP TIME 10 MIN **COOK TIME** 20 MIN **SERVINGS** 4

INGREDIENTS:

- 2 cups pumpkin, peeled and thinly sliced
- 1/2 cup walnuts, chopped
- 2 tbsp olive oil
- 1 clove garlic, minced
- 1/2 tsp ground cinnamon
- 1/2 tsp ground nutmeg
- Salt and pepper to taste
- Fresh parsley, chopped (for garnish)

INSTRUCTIONS:

1. Preheat oven to 400°F (200°C).
2. Toss pumpkin with olive oil, cinnamon, nutmeg, salt, and pepper. Spread on a baking sheet.
3. Bake for 20 minutes, turning halfway, until tender.
4. Toast walnuts in a skillet for 2-3 minutes. Add garlic and cook for 1 minute.
5. Transfer pumpkin to a serving dish. Top with walnuts and garlic. Garnish with parsley.

NUTRITIONAL FACTS (PER SERVING): *Calories: 180, Carbohydrates: 14g, Protein: 3g, Fat: 15g, Fiber: 3g*

FUN FACTS AND HEALTH BENEFIT:

Pumpkins are technically a fruit, and they belong to the same family as cucumbers and melons.

Pumpkin is rich in vitamin A, which supports good vision and a healthy immune system.

Baba Ganoush

V | GF

PREP TIME 10 MIN **COOK TIME** 20 MIN **SERVINGS** 4

INGREDIENTS:

- 2 medium eggplants
- 2 cloves garlic, minced
- 2 tbsp tahini
- 2 tbsp lemon juice
- 2 tbsp olive oil
- Salt and pepper to taste
- Chopped parsley for garnish
- Pita bread or vegetables for serving

INSTRUCTIONS:

1. Preheat oven to 400°F (200°C).
2. Pierce eggplants and place on parchment-lined baking sheet.
3. Roast for 20 mins until soft.
4. Cool slightly, then peel off skin.
5. Discard skin.
6. Blend eggplant, garlic, tahini, lemon juice, olive oil, salt, and pepper until smooth.
7. Transfer to serving bowl.
8. Garnish with parsley and drizzle with olive oil.
9. Serve with pita or veggies.

NUTRITIONAL FACTS (PER SERVING): *Calories: 80, Carbohydrates: 6g, Protein: 2g, Fat: 6g, Fiber: 3g*

FUN FACTS AND HEALTH BENEFIT:

The name "Baba Ganoush" is derived from Arabic, meaning "pampered father."

This dip is rich in fiber and antioxidants, supporting digestive health and reducing inflammation.

Moroccan Baked Brie   V

PREP TIME 3 MIN **COOK TIME** 10-12 MIN **SERVINGS** 6

INGREDIENTS:

- 1 wheel of Brie cheese
- 2 tbsp honey
- 1/4 cup sliced almonds
- Fresh rosemary sprigs for garnish
- Crackers or baguette slices for serving

INSTRUCTIONS:

1 Preheat oven to 350°F.
2 Place Brie on dish.
3 Drizzle with honey.
4 Sprinkle with almonds.
5 Bake for 10-12 mins.
6 Garnish with rosemary, serve warm with crackers.

NUTRITIONAL FACTS (PER SERVING): *Calories: 150, Carbohydrates: 8g, Protein: 6g, Fat: 11g, Fiber: 1g*

FUN FACTS AND HEALTH BENEFIT:

Moroccan Baked Brie is a tantalizing twist on the classic French cheese, infusing it with the exotic flavors of Morocco.

This dish elevates any gathering with its rich flavors and luxurious appeal, inviting guests on a culinary journey that transcends borders.

Turkish Lahmacun

PREP TIME 15 MIN **COOK TIME** 15 MIN **SERVINGS** 4

INGREDIENTS:

- 1 lb (450g) ground lamb/beef
- 1 onion, finely chopped
- 2 tomatoes, finely chopped
- 2 cloves garlic
- 2 tbsp tomato paste
- 2 tbsp olive oil
- 1 tbsp paprika
- 1 tsp ground cumin
- Salt and pepper to taste
- 4 flatbreads or tortillas
- Chopped parsley and lemon wedges

INSTRUCTIONS:

1 Preheat oven to 450°F (230°C).
2 Mix ground lamb/beef, onion, tomatoes, garlic, tomato paste, olive oil, paprika, cumin, salt, and pepper. Divide mixture into 4 portions.
3 Spread each portion on flatbread, leaving a border.
4 Place on parchment-lined baking sheet, bake for 12-15 mins until crispy. Sprinkle with parsley.
5 Serve hot with lemon wedges.

NUTRITIONAL FACTS (PER SERVING): *Calories: 250, Carbohydrates: 30g, Protein: 10g, Fat: 10g, Fiber: 2g*

FUN FACTS AND HEALTH BENEFIT:

Lahmacun is a popular Turkish street food. It is often referred to as "Turkish pizza,"

This dish is not only tasty but also provides a good balance of protein and carbohydrates, offering sustained energy and satiety.

Moroccan Spiced Carrot Dip V | GF

PREP TIME 15 MIN   **COOK TIME** 15 MIN   **SERVINGS** 6

INGREDIENTS:

· 4 large carrots
· 2 cloves garlic
· 2 tbsp olive oil
· 1 tsp ground cumin
· 1/2 tsp paprika
· 1/4 tsp ground cinnamon
· Fresh cilantro or parsley for garnish

INSTRUCTIONS:

1 Preheat oven to 200°C (400°F).
2 Toss chopped carrots with minced garlic, olive oil, cumin, paprika, cinnamon, salt, and pepper in a mixing bowl.
3 Spread seasoned carrots on a parchment-lined baking sheet. Roast in the oven for 15-20 minutes until tender and caramelized.
4 Remove from oven and let cool slightly.
5 Transfer roasted carrots to a food processor and blend until smooth, adding water or olive oil if needed. Taste and adjust seasoning.
6 Transfer dip to a serving bowl, garnish with fresh cilantro or parsley.

NUTRITIONAL FACTS (PER SERVING): *Calories: 50, Carbohydrates: 6g, Protein: 1g, Fat: 3g, Fiber: 2g*

FUN FACTS AND HEALTH BENEFIT:

Moroccan Spiced Carrot Dip, known as "Zaalouk," is a flavorful and vibrant appetizer in Moroccan cuisine.

Carrots are rich in beta-carotene, vitamins, and minerals, while the spices in this dip offer antioxidant and anti-inflammatory properties.

Hummus with Crudité Platter V | GF

PREP TIME 15 MIN   **COOK TIME** 0 MIN   **SERVINGS** 2

INGREDIENTS:

· 1 can (15 oz) chickpeas (garbanzo beans), drained and rinsed
· 1/4 cup tahini
· 2 cloves garlic, minced
· Juice of 1 lemon
· 2 tbsp olive oil
· Assorted raw vegetables (such as carrots, cucumbers, bell peppers, cherry tomatoes, celery), washed and cut into sticks or slices

INSTRUCTIONS:

1 Blend chickpeas, tahini, garlic, lemon juice, olive oil, salt, and pepper in a food processor until smooth.
2 Add water or olive oil if too thick, blend until desired consistency.
3 Adjust seasoning to taste with salt, pepper, or lemon juice.
4 Transfer hummus to a serving bowl, drizzle with olive oil.
5 Arrange raw vegetables around hummus on a platter. Serve immediately or refrigerate until ready to serve.

NUTRITIONAL FACTS (PER SERVING): *Calories: 100, Carbohydrates: 10g, Protein: 3g, Fat: 6g, Fiber: 4g*

FUN FACTS AND HEALTH BENEFIT:

Hummus has been enjoyed for centuries and is a staple in many Mediterranean diets.

This dish is rich in protein, fiber, and healthy fats, supporting heart health and keeping you feeling full longer.

CHAPTER 8

SOUPS

Discover the heartwarming flavors of Mediterranean soups, offering a blend of comforting and nourishing recipes perfect for any day.

Immerse yourself in the soothing embrace of Mediterranean soups, where each bowl is a warm, nourishing hug for your body and soul.

TIPS:

· Elevate your soups with a rich foundation of aromatics like onions, garlic, and leeks for unparalleled depth of flavor.

· Enhance your soups with a variety of beans, legumes, and grains, adding hearty protein and satisfying texture.

· Brighten your soup with a squeeze of fresh lemon juice, infusing a burst of vibrant flavor.

· Prepare in advance and freeze your soups, ensuring a quick and comforting meal is always at hand for busy days.

Avgolemono Soup

PREP TIME 10 MIN **COOK TIME** 20 MIN **SERVINGS** 4

INGREDIENTS:

· *6 cups chicken broth*
· *1/2 cup uncooked orzo pasta*
· *2 eggs*
· *1/2 cup pre-cooked or rotisserie chicken*
· *Juice of 1-2 lemons*
· *Salt and pepper to taste*
· *Chopped fresh dill for garnish*

INSTRUCTIONS:

1 In a large pot, bring chicken broth to a boil.
2 Add orzo pasta and cook according to package instructions until al dente. In a bowl, whisk together eggs and lemon juice until smooth.
3 Gradually add a ladleful of hot broth to the egg mixture, whisking constantly to temper the eggs.
4 Slowly pour the tempered egg mixture into the pot of soup, stirring constantly.
5 Shred chicken with a fork and add it to the soup pot.
6 Continue to cook for 2-3 minutes until the soup thickens slightly and chicken is heated through. Season to taste and garnish with chopped fresh dill.

NUTRITIONAL FACTS (PER SERVING): *Calories: 150, Carbohydrates: 10g, Protein: 8g, Fat: 8g, Fiber: 1g*

FUN FACTS AND HEALTH BENEFIT:

Avgolemono Soup, is a traditional Greek dish which translates to "egg-lemon," highlighting its distinctive ingredients.

This soup offers a boost of vitamin C and protein, supporting immune function and muscle repair.

Green Lentil Soup

V | GF

PREP TIME 10 MIN **COOK TIME** 20 MIN **SERVINGS** 4

INGREDIENTS:

· *1 cup green lentils, rinsed*
· *2 tbsp olive oil*
· *1 onion, chopped*
· *2 cloves garlic*
· *2 carrots, chopped*
· *2 celery stalks, chopped*
· *1 can (14 oz) diced tomatoes*
· *4 cups vegetable broth*
· *1 tsp ground cumin*
· *1 tsp ground coriander*
· *Fresh cilantro, chopped*

INSTRUCTIONS:

1 Sauté onion, garlic, carrots, celery in olive oil.
2 Add lentils, diced tomatoes, broth, cumin, coriander. Bring to boil.
3 Simmer until lentils are tender, about 20 mins.
4 Season with salt, pepper.
5 Serve hot, garnish with cilantro.

NUTRITIONAL FACTS (PER SERVING): *Calories: 250, Carbohydrates: 35g, Protein: 12g, Fat: 8g, Fiber: 12g*

FUN FACTS AND HEALTH BENEFIT:

Lentils have been a staple food for thousands of years, dating back to ancient civilizations like the Egyptians and Mesopotamians.

A hearty and nutritious dish rich in fiber, protein, and essential vitamins, promoting digestive health and providing sustained energy.

Fish and Okra Soup GF

PREP TIME 10 MIN   **COOK TIME** 20 MIN   **SERVINGS** 4

INGREDIENTS:

- 1 lb white fish fillets (such as cod or tilapia), cut into chunks
- 1 cup okra, sliced
- 2 tbsp olive oil
- 1 onion, chopped
- 2 cloves garlic, minced
- 1 can (14 oz) diced tomatoes
- 4 cups fish broth or water
- 1 tsp smoked paprika
- Salt and pepper to taste
- Fresh cilantro or parsley for garnish

INSTRUCTIONS:

1 Sauté onion, garlic in olive oil.
2 Add tomatoes, broth, paprika, cayenne, salt, pepper. Simmer.
3 Add okra, cook for 10 mins.
4 Add fish, simmer until cooked, about 5-7 mins.
5 Serve hot, garnish with cilantro or parsley.

NUTRITIONAL FACTS (PER SERVING): *Calories: 200, Carbohydrates: 10g, Protein: 25g, Fat: 8g, Fiber: 3g*

FUN FACTS AND HEALTH BENEFIT:

Okra, also known as "lady's fingers," is prized for its unique texture and mucilaginous properties, which help to thicken soups and stews.

With origins from North Africa, this soup is packed with omega-3 fatty acids and antioxidants, supporting heart health and inflammation reduction.

Moroccan Vegetable Soup V | GF

PREP TIME 10 MIN   **COOK TIME** 20 MIN   **SERVINGS** 4

INGREDIENTS:

- 2 tbsp olive oil
- 1 onion, chopped
- 2 cloves garlic, minced
- 2 carrots, chopped
- 2 celery stalks, chopped
- 1 zucchini
- 1 can (14 oz) diced tomatoes
- 4 cups vegetable broth
- 1 can (15 oz) chickpeas
- 1 tsp ground cumin
- 1 tsp ground coriander
- 1 tsp ground turmeric
- Fresh cilantro

INSTRUCTIONS:

1 Sauté onion, garlic, carrots, and celery in olive oil.
2 Add cumin, coriander, turmeric, tomatoes, broth, and chickpeas. Bring to a boil.
3 Add zucchini, simmer until tender, about 10 mins. Season with salt and pepper.
4 Serve hot, garnish with cilantro.

NUTRITIONAL FACTS (PER SERVING): *Calories: 220, Carbohydrates: 35g, Protein: 8g, Fat: 8g, Fiber: 10g*

FUN FACTS AND HEALTH BENEFIT:

Moroccan vegetable soup, also known as "Harira," is commonly enjoyed during Ramadan to break the fast, symbolizing nourishment and community.

A vibrant blend of spices and vegetables, it offers a rich source of antioxidants and fiber, promoting overall health and immune support.

Broccoli and Almond Soup V | GF

PREP TIME 10 MIN   **COOK TIME** 20 MIN   **SERVINGS** 4

INGREDIENTS:

· 2 tbsp olive oil
· 1 onion, chopped
· 2 cloves garlic, minced
· 1 lb broccoli florets
· 4 cups vegetable broth
· 1/2 cup ground almonds
· 1/2 cup almond milk
· Salt and pepper to taste

INSTRUCTIONS:

1 Sauté onion and garlic until soft.
2 Add broccoli and broth, simmer until tender.
3 Blend until smooth.
4 Stir in ground almonds and almond milk.
5 Season with salt and pepper.
6 Serve hot.

NUTRITIONAL FACTS (PER SERVING): *Calories: 250, Carbohydrates: 18g, Protein: 8g, Fat: 18g, Fiber: 6g*

FUN FACTS AND HEALTH BENEFIT:

Broccoli Soup is a powerhouse of nutrients. Broccoli belongs to the cruciferous vegetable family, known for its cancer-fighting properties.

This soup is packed with vitamins, minerals, and healthy fats, supporting bone health and cognitive function.

Pasta and Bean Soup V

PREP TIME 10 MIN   **COOK TIME** 20 MIN   **SERVINGS** 4

INGREDIENTS:

· 2 tbsp olive oil
· 1 onion, chopped
· 2 cloves garlic, minced
· 2 carrots
· 2 celery stalks
· 1 can (14 oz) diced tomatoes
· 1 cup small pasta
· 1 can (14 oz) cannellini beans
· 4 cups vegetable or chicken broth
· 1 tsp dried oregano
· 1 tsp dried basil
· Fresh parsley

INSTRUCTIONS:

1 Sauté onion, garlic, carrots, and celery in olive oil until softened.
2 Stir in diced tomatoes and cannellini beans; cook for 2-3 minutes.
3 Add broth, oregano, and basil; simmer for 10 mins. Cook pasta in the pot until al dente, about 8-10 minutes.
4 Season with salt and pepper, then serve hot with fresh parsley and grated Parmesan cheese.

NUTRITIONAL FACTS (PER SERVING): *Calories: 250, Carbohydrates: 40g, Protein: 10g, Fat: 6g, Fiber: 8g*

FUN FACTS AND HEALTH BENEFIT:

Pasta and Bean Soup, also known as "Pasta e Fagioli," is a beloved Italian dating back to ancient Rome where it was originally a humble peasant dish.

It is rich in fiber and plant-based protein, promoting digestive health and sustained energy levels.

French Soupe au Pistou

V | GF

PREP TIME 10 MIN   **COOK TIME** 20 MIN   **SERVINGS** 4

INGREDIENTS:

- 2 tbsp olive oil
- 1 onion, chopped
- 2 cloves garlic, minced
- 2 carrots, chopped
- 2 zucchini, chopped
- 1 can (14 oz) diced tomatoes
- 4 cups vegetable broth
- 1 cup green beans, trimmed and cut into 1-inch pieces
- 1 can (15 oz) white beans, drained and rinsed
- 1/2 cup pesto
- Fresh basil

INSTRUCTIONS:

1 Sauté onion and garlic until softened.
2 Add carrots, zucchini, diced tomatoes with juice, and vegetable broth, bring to a boil.
3 Add green beans and white beans, simmer until vegetables are tender.
4 Season with salt and pepper.
5 Serve hot, stir in pesto, and garnish with fresh basil.

NUTRITIONAL FACTS (PER SERVING): *Calories: 250, Carbohydrates: 30g, Protein: 8g, Fat: 12g, Fiber: 6g*

FUN FACTS AND HEALTH BENEFIT:

French Soupe au Pistou is a Provencal vegetable soup flavored with a fragrant basil and garlic paste called "pistou."

This soup offers a burst of antioxidants and essential nutrients, enhancing overall vitality and immune resilience.

Italian White Bean and Kale Soup

V | GF

PREP TIME 10 MIN   **COOK TIME** 20 MIN   **SERVINGS** 4

INGREDIENTS:

- 2 tbsp olive oil
- 1 onion, chopped
- 2 cloves garlic, minced
- 2 carrots, chopped
- 2 celery stalks, chopped
- 1 can (14 oz) white beans, drained and rinsed
- 4 cups vegetable broth
- 2 cups chopped kale
- 1 tsp dried thyme
- Salt and pepper to taste

INSTRUCTIONS:

1 Sauté onion, garlic, carrots, and celery until tender.
2 Stir in white beans, vegetable broth, and dried thyme, bring to a boil.
3 Add chopped kale, simmer until tender.
4 Season with salt and pepper.
5 Serve hot, garnish with Parmesan cheese if desired.

NUTRITIONAL FACTS (PER SERVING): *Calories: 200, Carbohydrates: 30g, Protein: 8g, Fat: 6g, Fiber: 8g*

FUN FACTS AND HEALTH BENEFIT:

Italian White Bean and Kale Soup, known as "Ribollita." translates to "reboiled." This soup was traditionally made by reheating leftover minestrone soup and adding bread.

This dish provides a robust source of fiber, vitamins, and minerals, supporting immune function and heart health.

Italian Tomato Basil Soup   V | GF

PREP TIME 10 MIN   **COOK TIME** 30 MIN   **SERVINGS** 6

INGREDIENTS:

· 2 tbsp olive oil
· 1 onion, chopped
· 3 cloves garlic, minced
· 28 oz canned crushed tomatoes
· 4 cups vegetable broth
· 1/4 cup fresh basil leaves, chopped
· Salt and pepper to taste
· 1/4 cup heavy cream (optional, for creamy version)

INSTRUCTIONS:

1   Sauté onion in olive oil until softened, about 5 mins. Add garlic and cook for 1-2 mins until fragrant.
2   Stir in crushed tomatoes and vegetable broth. Simmer for 20-25 mins.
3   Remove from heat, add chopped basil.
4   Blend soup until smooth using an immersion blender or in batches in a regular blender.
5   Season with salt and pepper. Add heavy cream if desired.
6   Serve hot, garnished with basil leaves.

NUTRITIONAL FACTS (PER SERVING): *Calories: 1084, Carbohydrates: 250g, Protein: 15g, Fat: 3g, Fiber: 15g*

FUN FACTS AND HEALTH BENEFIT:

Tomato basil soup is a classic Italian dish that celebrates the simplicity of fresh ingredients.

Tomatoes are rich in antioxidants like lycopene, which may help reduce the risk of chronic diseases.

Lebanese Lentil Soup   V | GF

PREP TIME 10 MIN   **COOK TIME** 20 MIN   **SERVINGS** 4

INGREDIENTS:

· 2 tbsp olive oil
· 1 onion, chopped
· 2 cloves garlic, minced
· 2 carrots, chopped
· 1 cup red lentils, rinsed
· 4 cups vegetable broth
· 1 tsp ground cumin
· 1 tsp ground coriander
· 1/2 tsp ground turmeric
· Salt and pepper to taste
· Fresh lemon wedges for serving
· Fresh parsley

INSTRUCTIONS:

1   Sauté onion and garlic until softened.
2   Add carrots, red lentils, vegetable broth, ground cumin, ground coriander, and ground turmeric, bring to a boil.
3   Simmer until lentils are tender.
4   Season with salt and pepper.
5   Serve hot, with fresh lemon wedges, garnished with fresh parsley.

NUTRITIONAL FACTS (PER SERVING): *Calories: 240, Carbohydrates: 35g, Protein: 12g, Fat: 8g, Fiber: 12g*

FUN FACTS AND HEALTH BENEFIT:

Lebanese lentil soup, known as Shorbat Adas, is a staple dish in Lebanese cuisine. In Lebanese households, serving lentil soup to guests symbolizes hospitality.

This soup provides a rich source of plant-based protein, fiber, and essential nutrients, supporting overall health and well-being.

CHAPTER 9

SALADS

Explore vibrant, nutritious salads bursting with fresh vegetables, proteins, and unique dressings to elevate your meals effortlessly.

Tuck into the world of fresh greens where a myriad of luscious ingredients and dressings blend to create an invigorating feast for the body, mind and soul.

TIPS:

· Use a variety of colorful vegetables to create visually appealing salads.

· Don't be afraid to add protein like grilled chicken, salmon, or chickpeas for added depth.

· Experiment with different citrus juices and olive oils for unique flavor combinations.

· Have you experimented and found your favorite dressing? Make a bigger batch and store it for use over multiple meals.

Couscous Salad

V

PREP TIME 10 MIN **COOK TIME** 5 MIN **SERVINGS** 4

INGREDIENTS:

· 1 cup couscous
· 1 1/4 cups vegetable broth or water
· 1 cup chopped cucumber
· 1 cup chopped tomatoes
· 1/2 cup chopped red onion
· 1/4 cup chopped fresh parsley
· 1/4 cup chopped fresh mint
· 2 tbsp extra virgin olive oil
· 2 tbsp fresh lemon juice

INSTRUCTIONS:

1 Boil vegetable broth or water in saucepan. Stir in couscous, cover, remove from heat, let stand for 5 mins. Fluff couscous with fork, transfer to large bowl.
2 Add chopped cucumber, tomatoes, red onion, parsley, and mint to bowl.
3 Whisk olive oil, lemon juice, salt, and pepper in small bowl for dressing.
4 Drizzle dressing over salad, toss to coat.

NUTRITIONAL FACTS (PER SERVING): *Calories: 200, Carbohydrates: 35g, Protein: 6g, Fat: 5g, Fiber: 4g*

FUN FACTS AND HEALTH BENEFIT:

Despite its grain-like appearance, couscous is actually tiny steamed balls of crushed durum wheat semolina.

This nutritious salad provides a good source of fiber, vitamins, and minerals, supporting digestive health and sustained energy levels.

Turkish Ezme

V | GF

PREP TIME 15 MIN **COOK TIME** 0 MIN **SERVINGS** 4

INGREDIENTS:

· 4 medium tomatoes,
· 1 medium cucumber,
· 1 green bell pepper,
· 1 red onion, finely diced
· 2 cloves garlic, minced
· 1/4 cup fresh parsley,
· 2 tbsp fresh mint, finely chopped
· 2 tbsp olive oil
· 1 tbsp pomegranate molasses (optional)
· 1 tbsp lemon juice
· 1 tsp red pepper flakes

INSTRUCTIONS:

1 In a large mixing bowl, combine diced tomatoes, cucumber, green bell pepper, red onion, garlic, parsley, and mint.
2 Add olive oil, pomegranate molasses (if using), lemon juice, red pepper flakes, salt, and pepper.
3 Mix thoroughly until all ingredients are well combined. Adjust seasoning to taste.
4 Let the salad sit for at least 15 minutes to allow the flavors to meld. Serve as a side dish.

NUTRITIONAL FACTS (PER SERVING): *Calories: 100, Carbohydrates: 10g, Protein: 2g, Fat: 7g, Fiber: 3g*

FUN FACTS AND HEALTH BENEFIT:

Ezme is a popular Turkish condiment often served with grilled meats and kebabs, known for its spicy and tangy flavor.

The fresh vegetables in Ezme salad provide a rich source of vitamins, minerals, and antioxidants, supporting overall health and wellness.

Asparagus and Orange Salad

V | GF

PREP TIME 10 MIN **COOK TIME** 5 MIN **SERVINGS** 4

INGREDIENTS:

· *1 bunch asparagus trimmed and blanched*
· *2 sliced oranges*
· *2 tbsp extra virgin olive oil*
· *1 tbsp red wine vinegar*
· *1 tsp Dijon mustard*
· *1 clove garlic, minced*
· *Salt and pepper to taste*

INSTRUCTIONS:

1 Arrange blanched asparagus spears and orange slices on a serving platter.
2 In a small bowl, whisk together extra virgin olive oil, red wine vinegar, Dijon mustard, minced garlic, salt, and pepper to make the vinaigrette.
3 Drizzle the vinaigrette over the salad.
4 Serve immediately as a light and refreshing appetizer or side dish.
5 Enjoy!

NUTRITIONAL FACTS (PER SERVING): *Calories: 80, Carbohydrates: 10g, Protein: 3g, Fat: 5g, Fiber: 4g*

FUN FACTS AND HEALTH BENEFIT:

Asparagus is believed to have been cultivated by the ancient Egyptians over 5,000 years ago, and was prized by ancient Greeks and Romans for its medicinal properties.

This salad provides a wealth of vitamins, fiber, and antioxidants, promoting digestive health and overall well-being.

Avocado, Orange, Almond Salad

V | GF

PREP TIME 10 MIN **COOK TIME** 0 MIN **SERVINGS** 4

INGREDIENTS:

· *2 ripe avocados, peeled, pitted, and diced*
· *2 oranges, peeled and segmented*
· *1/4 cup sliced almonds, toasted*
· *Add a bed of spinach if preferred*
· *2 tbsp extra virgin olive oil*
· *1 tbsp fresh lemon juice*
· *1 tsp honey (optional)*
· *Salt and pepper to taste*

INSTRUCTIONS:

1 In a large bowl, combine diced avocados, orange segments, and toasted sliced almonds.
2 In a small bowl, whisk together extra virgin olive oil, fresh lemon juice, honey (if using), salt, and pepper to make the dressing.
3 Drizzle the dressing over the salad and gently toss to coat evenly.
4 Serve immediately as a refreshing and nutritious appetizer or side dish.

NUTRITIONAL FACTS (PER SERVING): *Calories: 200, Carbohydrates: 15g, Protein: 4g, Fat: 15g, Fiber: 6g*

FUN FACTS AND HEALTH BENEFIT:

Avocados are often called "nature's butter" due to their rich, creamy texture.

This salad provides healthy fats, vitamins, and antioxidants, supporting heart health and glowing skin.

Italian Panzanella Salad   V

PREP TIME 15 MIN   **COOK TIME** 0 MIN   **SERVINGS** 4

INGREDIENTS:

- 4 cups stale bread, cubed
- 2 large tomatoes, chopped
- 1 cucumber, sliced
- 1 red onion, thinly sliced
- 1/2 cup Kalamata olives, pitted
- 1/4 cup fresh basil leaves, torn
- 2 tbsp capers, drained
- 1/4 cup extra virgin olive oil
- 2 tbsp red wine vinegar
- Salt and pepper to taste

INSTRUCTIONS:

1 Toss bread cubes with olive oil.
2 Combine with tomatoes, cucumber, onion, olives, basil, and capers.
3 Whisk olive oil, vinegar, salt, and pepper for dressing.
4 Pour dressing over salad, toss gently.
5 Rest for 10 mins.
6 Serve or refrigerate.

NUTRITIONAL FACTS (PER SERVING): *Calories: 320, Carbohydrates: 35g, Protein: 6g, Fat: 18g, Fiber: 5g*

FUN FACTS AND HEALTH BENEFIT:

In the 16th century, panzanella was considered a dish for the poor. Its name derives from "pan," meaning bread, highlighting its key ingredient.

This salad provides fiber, vitamins, and antioxidants, supporting digestive health and reducing inflammation.

Mediterranean Quinoa Salad   V | GF

PREP TIME 15 MIN   **COOK TIME** 15 MIN   **SERVINGS** 4

INGREDIENTS:

- 1 cup quinoa
- 2 cups water
- 1 cup cherry tomatoes, halved
- 1 cucumber, diced
- 1/4 cup crumbled feta cheese
- 1/2 cup Kalamata olives, pitted and sliced
- 2 tbsp olive oil
- 2 tbsp lemon juice
- 1 clove garlic
- 1 tsp dried oregano

INSTRUCTIONS:

1 In a medium saucepan, bring quinoa and water to a boil. Reduce heat to low, cover, and simmer for 12-15 minutes or until quinoa is tender and water is absorbed. Fluff quinoa with a fork.
2 In a large bowl, combine cooked quinoa, cherry tomatoes, diced cucumber, sliced Kalamata olives, and crumbled feta cheese.
3 In a small bowl, whisk together extra virgin olive oil, fresh lemon juice, minced garlic, dried oregano, salt, and pepper to make the dressing.
4 Drizzle the dressing over the salad and toss to coat evenly. Serve chilled.

NUTRITIONAL FACTS (PER SERVING): *Calories: 220, Carbohydrates: 25g, Protein: 8g, Fat: 10g, Fiber: 5g*

FUN FACTS AND HEALTH BENEFIT:

Quinoa was considered "the gold of the Incas" due to its high nutritional value.

This salad offers a complete protein source and also add fiber, vitamins, and antioxidants, supporting heart health and boosting energy levels.

Greek Salad
V | GF

PREP TIME 10 MIN **COOK TIME** 0 MIN **SERVINGS** 4

INGREDIENTS:

- 2 large tomatoes, chopped
- 1 cucumber, chopped
- 1 red onion, thinly sliced
- 1 green bell pepper, chopped
- 1/2 cup Kalamata olives, pitted
- 1/2 cup crumbled feta cheese
- 2 tbsp extra virgin olive oil
- 1 tbsp lemon juice
- 1 tsp dried oregano
- alt and pepper to taste

INSTRUCTIONS:

1 In a large bowl, combine chopped tomatoes, cucumber, red onion, green bell pepper, Kalamata olives, and crumbled feta cheese.

2 In a small bowl, whisk together extra virgin olive oil, fresh lemon juice, dried oregano, salt, and pepper to make the dressing.

3 Drizzle the dressing over the salad and toss to coat evenly. Serve immediately.

NUTRITIONAL FACTS (PER SERVING): *Calories: 120, Carbohydrates: 6g, Protein: 3g, Fat: 10g, Fiber: 2g*

FUN FACTS AND HEALTH BENEFIT:

The salad's ingredients reflect the colors of the Greek flag—white from feta cheese, blue from olives, and green from cucumbers and lettuce.

This dish provides a rich source of vitamins, antioxidants, and healthy fats, supporting overall health and vitality.

Salad Nicoise
GF

PREP TIME 15 MIN **COOK TIME** 0 MIN **SERVINGS** 4

INGREDIENTS:

- 8 oz (225g) canned tuna,
- 4 boiled potatoes, halved
- 1 cup cooked green beans
- 4 hard-boiled eggs, halved
- 2 tomatoes, sliced
- 4 cups mixed salad greens
- 2 tbsp red wine vinegar
- 1/4 cup extra virgin olive oil
- 1 tsp Dijon mustard
- 1/2 cup Kalamata olives, pitted

INSTRUCTIONS:

1 Arrange mixed salad greens on a large serving platter. Top with canned tuna, boiled potatoes, cooked green beans, hard-boiled eggs, tomato slices, and Kalamata olives.

2 In a small bowl, whisk together red wine vinegar, extra virgin olive oil, Dijon mustard, salt, and pepper to make the vinaigrette.

3 Drizzle the vinaigrette over the salad.

4 Serve immediately.

NUTRITIONAL FACTS (PER SERVING): *Calories: 350, Carbohydrates: 15g, Protein: 25g, Fat: 20g, Fiber: 6g*

FUN FACTS AND HEALTH BENEFIT:

Salad Niçoise originated in the city of Nice, France, as a hearty meal for fishermen.

This salad provides protein, vitamins, and omega-3 fatty acids, supporting heart health and satiety.

Spanish Chorizo and Avocado Salad

GF

PREP TIME 10 MIN **COOK TIME** 10 MIN **SERVINGS** 4

INGREDIENTS:

· 2 ripe avocados, peeled, pitted, and sliced
· 200g (7 oz) Spanish chorizo, sliced
· 1 cup cherry tomatoes, halved
· 1/4 red onion, thinly sliced
· 2 cups mixed salad greens
· 2 tbsp extra-virgin olive oil
· 1 tbsp balsamic vinegar
· Salt and pepper to taste

INSTRUCTIONS:

1 Cook chorizo until crispy, set aside.
2 Whisk olive oil and balsamic vinegar for dressing.
3 Combine avocados, cherry tomatoes, red onion, and greens in a salad bowl.
4 Add cooked chorizo.
5 Drizzle dressing, toss gently.
6 Serve immediately, garnish with salt and pepper.

NUTRITIONAL FACTS (PER SERVING): *Calories: 400, Carbohydrates: 50g, Protein: 20g, Fat: 30g, Fiber: 5g*

FUN FACTS AND HEALTH BENEFIT:

Chorizo's vibrant red color comes from paprika, which contains capsaicin, known for boosting metabolism.

This salad offers a balance of spicy and creamy flavors while providing essential nutrients, promoting cardiovascular health and satiety.

Moroccan Carrot and Chickpea Salad

V | GF

PREP TIME 15 MIN **COOK TIME** 0 MIN **SERVINGS** 4

INGREDIENTS:

· 4 large carrots
· 1 can (400g/14 oz) chickpeas, drained and rinsed
· 1/4 cup chopped fresh parsley
· 1/4 cup chopped fresh cilantro
· 1 tbsp lemon juice
· 1 tsp ground cumin
· 1/2 tsp ground cinnamon
· 1/4 tsp ground turmeric
· 2 tbsp extra-virgin olive oil
· Salt and pepper to taste

INSTRUCTIONS:

1 Combine grated carrots, chickpeas, parsley, and cilantro in a mixing bowl.
2 Whisk olive oil, lemon juice, cumin, cinnamon, turmeric, salt, and pepper in a small bowl for dressing. Pour dressing over carrot and chickpea mixture, toss gently.
3 Let salad marinate for at least 10 minutes.
4 Serve chilled or at room temperature, garnished with additional parsley or cilantro if desired.

NUTRITIONAL FACTS (PER SERVING): *Calories: 300, Carbohydrates: 45g, Protein: 10g, Fat: 10g, Fiber: 10g*

FUN FACTS AND HEALTH BENEFIT:

Moroccan Carrot and Chickpea Salad is a delightful example of how traditional Moroccan cuisine combines sweet and savory elements.

This salad provides a rich source of fiber, vitamins, and antioxidants, supporting digestive health and immune function.

Sardinian Fennel and Orange Salad

V | GF

PREP TIME 15 MIN **COOK TIME** 0 MIN **SERVINGS** 4

INGREDIENTS:

- 2 large oranges, peeled and segmented
- 1 large fennel bulb, thinly sliced
- 1/4 cup black olives, pitted and halved
- 1/4 red onion, thinly sliced
- 2 tbsp fresh parsley, chopped
- 2 tbsp extra virgin olive oil
- 1 tbsp white wine vinegar
- Salt and pepper to taste

INSTRUCTIONS:

1 Prep citrus: Peel and segment oranges.
2 Slice fennel and place in bowl.
3 Add oranges, olives, and onion to fennel.
4 Whisk oil, vinegar, salt, and pepper.
5 Pour dressing over salad, add parsley, toss, and serve.

NUTRITIONAL FACTS (PER SERVING): *Calories: 120, Carbohydrates: 12g, Protein: 2g, Fat: 8g, Fiber: 3g*

FUN FACTS AND HEALTH BENEFIT:

Fennel has been used since ancient times for its medicinal properties and was believed to convey longevity.

This vibrant salad provides vitamins, fiber, and antioxidants, promoting digestive health and immune function.

Aegean Watermelon and Olive Salad

V | GF

PREP TIME 10 MIN **COOK TIME** 0 MIN **SERVINGS** 4

INGREDIENTS:

- 4 cups watermelon, cubed
- 1/2 cup crumbled feta cheese
- 1/4 cup Kalamata olives, pitted and halved
- 1 small red onion, thinly sliced
- 1/4 cup fresh mint leaves, chopped
- 1/4 cup fresh basil leaves, torn
- 2 tbsp extra virgin olive oil
- 1 tbsp balsamic glaze
- Salt and pepper to taste

INSTRUCTIONS:

1 Cube the watermelon, crumble the feta cheese, halve the olives, and thinly slice the red onion.
2 Combine watermelon, feta, olives, red onion, chopped mint, and torn basil in a large bowl.
3 Drizzle olive oil and balsamic glaze over the salad.
4 Gently toss to combine, season with salt and pepper to taste, and serve immediately.

NUTRITIONAL FACTS (PER SERVING): *Calories: 150, Carbohydrates: 15g, Protein: 4g, Fat: 9g, Fiber: 2g*

FUN FACTS AND HEALTH BENEFIT:

Watermelon is over 90% water, making it one of the most hydrating fruits.

This salad provides hydration and electrolytes, supporting overall hydration and promoting skin health.

CHAPTER 10

VEGETABLES

Celebrate the vibrant flavors of Mediterranean dinners, featuring seasonal vegetables and simple techniques to elevate your meals with natural sweetness and depth.

Let the Mediterranean garden spark your culinary adventure, turning every veggie into a brushstroke of flavor and exuberance.

TIPS:

· Use a variety of colorful vegetables to add visual appeal and nutritional value to your dishes.

· Avoid overcooking – Mediterranean vegetables are best enjoyed tender but still crisp, preserving their natural flavors and textures.

· Roast your vegetables to bring out their natural sweetness, creating a delicious and easy side dish.

· Enhance your vegetables with a drizzle of high-quality olive oil and a sprinkle of sea salt to elevate their natural flavors.

Sautéed Collard Greens V | GF

PREP TIME 10 MIN **COOK TIME** 10 MIN **SERVINGS** 4

INGREDIENTS:

- 1 bunch collard greens, stemmed and chopped
- 2 tbsp olive oil
- 2 cloves garlic, minced
- 1/2 tsp red pepper flakes
- Salt and pepper to taste
- 1 tbsp lemon juice

INSTRUCTIONS:

1 Sauté garlic and red pepper flakes in olive oil.
2 Add collard greens; cook until tender.
3 Season with salt, pepper, and lemon juice.
4 Serve hot.

NUTRITIONAL FACTS (PER SERVING): *Calories: 100, Carbohydrates: 10g, Protein: 3g, Fat: 7g, Fiber: 5g*

FUN FACTS AND HEALTH BENEFIT:

Collard greens likely originated in the eastern Mediterranean, where ancient Greeks and Romans cultivated and consumed them as a nutritious and versatile vegetable.

This dish provides a powerhouse of vitamins, minerals, and antioxidants, supporting bone health and reducing inflammation.

Grilled Asparagus with Lemon V | GF

PREP TIME 10 MIN **COOK TIME** 10 MIN **SERVINGS** 4

INGREDIENTS:

- 1 bunch asparagus, woody ends trimmed
- 2 tbsp extra virgin olive oil
- 1 tbsp lemon juice
- 1 tsp lemon zest
- Salt and pepper to taste

INSTRUCTIONS:

1 Preheat grill to medium-high.
2 Whisk olive oil, lemon juice, zest, salt, and pepper for marinade.
3 Place asparagus in dish, drizzle with marinade, toss to coat.
4 Grill asparagus for 5-7 mins, turning occasionally, until tender and charred.
5 Transfer to platter.
6 Serve hot or at room temp as side or appetizer.

NUTRITIONAL FACTS (PER SERVING): *Calories: 60, Carbohydrates: 5g, Protein: 3g, Fat: 4g, Fiber: 3g*

FUN FACTS AND HEALTH BENEFIT:

Asparagus contains high levels of glutathione, a powerful antioxidant that supports liver health.

This dish provides vitamins, fiber, and antioxidants, promoting digestive health and reducing oxidative stress.

Broccoli di Rabe

V | GF

PREP TIME 10 MIN **COOK TIME** 10 MIN **SERVINGS** 4

INGREDIENTS:

- 1 bunch broccoli rabe, trimmed and chopped
- 2 tbsp olive oil
- 3 cloves garlic, thinly sliced
- 1/4 tsp red pepper flakes
- Salt and pepper to taste
- Fresh lemon wedges for serving
- Grated Parmesan cheese for serving

INSTRUCTIONS:

1 Boil salted water. Blanch broccoli rabe 2 mins.
2 Drain and ice bath (to cool down rapidly).
3 Heat oil in skillet.
4 Sauté garlic and red pepper 1 min.
5 Add broccoli rabe; cook 5-7 mins.
6 Season with salt and pepper.
7 Transfer to dish.
8 Add lemon juice and Parmesan.
9 Serve hot as side dish.

NUTRITIONAL FACTS (PER SERVING): *Calories: 50, Carbohydrates: 6g, Protein: 3g, Fat: 3g, Fiber: 3g*

FUN FACTS AND HEALTH BENEFIT:

Broccoli di Rabe, a staple in Italian cooking, offers a taste of culinary tradition. It was cultivated by ancient Romans and has been enjoyed for centuries.

Its high vitamin A content boosts immunity and collagen production, enhancing skin health and wound healing.

Turkish Eggplant Salad

V | GF

PREP TIME 10 MIN **COOK TIME** 20 MIN **SERVINGS** 4

INGREDIENTS:

- 2 large eggplants
- 2 cloves garlic, minced
- 1/2 cup plain Greek yogurt
- 2 tbsp extra virgin olive oil
- 1 tbsp fresh lemon juice
- 1 tsp ground cumin
- Salt and pepper to taste
- Chopped fresh parsley for garnish
- 1/4 cup diced tomatoes for garnish
- 1/4 cup diced green peppers for garnish
- 1/2 tsp sesame seeds for garnish

INSTRUCTIONS:

1 Preheat oven to 400°F (200°C).
2 Place whole eggplants on parchment-lined baking sheet.
3 Roast for 20 mins until skins charred and flesh is soft. Remove from oven, let cool.
4 Peel off the skins and discard.
5 Slice the roasted eggplant.
6 In the bowl, mix diced eggplant with minced garlic, Greek yogurt, olive oil, lemon juice, cumin, salt, and pepper.
7 Transfer to a serving dish, and garnish with the chopped parsley, diced tomatoes, sesame seeds and green pepper.

NUTRITIONAL FACTS (PER SERVING): *Calories: 90, Carbohydrates: 12g, Protein: 3g, Fat: 5g, Fiber: 4g*

FUN FACTS AND HEALTH BENEFIT:

Eggplants, native to the Indian subcontinent, traveled along the Silk Road to Turkey, becoming a staple in Turkish cuisine.

Eggplants are rich in antioxidants and fiber, supporting heart health and digestion.

Zucchini with Moroccan Spices

V | GF

PREP TIME 5 MIN **COOK TIME** 10 MIN **SERVINGS** 4

INGREDIENTS:

- 2 medium zucchinis, sliced
- 2 tbsp olive oil
- 1 tsp ground cumin
- 1/2 tsp ground coriander
- 1/2 tsp ground paprika
- 1/4 tsp ground cinnamon
- Salt and pepper to taste
- Fresh cilantro for garnish

INSTRUCTIONS:

1 Heat olive oil in skillet.
2 Add ground cumin, coriander, paprika, and cinnamon; cook until fragrant.
3 Add zucchini; cook until tender.
4 Season with salt and pepper.
5 Garnish with fresh cilantro; serve hot.

NUTRITIONAL FACTS (PER SERVING): *Calories: 120, Carbohydrates: 8g, Protein: 2g, Fat: 10g, Fiber: 2g*

FUN FACTS AND HEALTH BENEFIT:

Moroccan cuisine is renowned for its intricate spice blends, showcasing influences from Arab, Berber, and Mediterranean cultures.

Zucchini is low in calories and packed with vitamins, supporting overall health and well-being.

Turkish Cucumber Salad (Cacik)

V | GF

PREP TIME 10 MIN **COOK TIME** 0 MIN **SERVINGS** 4

INGREDIENTS:

- 2 cups plain yogurt
- 1 cucumber, grated or finely chopped
- 2 cloves garlic, minced
- 1 tbsp fresh dill, chopped
- 1 tbsp fresh mint, chopped
- 1 tbsp olive oil
- 1 tbsp lemon juice
- Salt and pepper to taste

INSTRUCTIONS:

1 In a mixing bowl, combine yogurt, grated cucumber, minced garlic, dill, mint, olive oil, and lemon juice.
2 Stir until well combined.
3 Season with salt and pepper to taste.
4 Chill in the refrigerator for at least 30 minutes before serving to allow flavors to meld (optional).
5 Serve cold as a side dish or appetizer with grilled chicken kebabs, fish, or alongside warm pita bread and hummus for a complete Mediterranean meal.

NUTRITIONAL FACTS (PER SERVING): *Calories: 120, Carbohydrates: 8g, Protein: 6g, Fat: 7g, Fiber: 1g*

FUN FACTS AND HEALTH BENEFIT:

Cacik is a traditional Turkish yogurt-based dish often served as a refreshing accompaniment to meals, particularly in hot weather.

Yogurt in cacik provides probiotics that support gut health and digestion, while cucumbers are hydrating.

Italian-Style Roasted Bell Peppers

V | GF

PREP TIME 10 MIN **COOK TIME** 20 MIN **SERVINGS** 4

INGREDIENTS:

· 4 bell peppers (any color), halved and seeded
· 2 cloves garlic, minced
· 2 tbsp extra virgin olive oil
· 1 tbsp balsamic vinegar
· 1 tsp dried oregano
· Salt and pepper to taste

INSTRUCTIONS:

1 Preheat oven to 400°F (200°C).
2 Place halved, seeded bell peppers cut side down on parchment-lined baking sheet.
3 Roast for 15 mins until skins blister and char.
4 After roasting, immediately transfer peppers to bowl, cover with plastic wrap, steam for 5 mins. Peel off skins, discard.
5 While steaming the peppers, slice peppers into strips, place in serving dish.
6 Whisk minced garlic, olive oil, balsamic vinegar, oregano, salt, and pepper for dressing.
7 Drizzle dressing over peppers, toss to coat.
8 Serve warm or at room temp as appetizer.

NUTRITIONAL FACTS (PER SERVING): *Calories: 100, Carbohydrates: 8g, Protein: 2g, Fat: 7g, Fiber: 3g*

FUN FACTS AND HEALTH BENEFIT:

Bell peppers, originating in Central and South America, reached Europe via Christopher Columbus. Initially ornamental, they became staples in Mediterranean cuisine. Rich in vitamin C, they aid immunity and skin health.

Spinach with Raisins and Pine Nuts

V | GF

PREP TIME 5 MIN **COOK TIME** 10 MIN **SERVINGS** 4

INGREDIENTS:

· 2 tbsp olive oil
· 2 cloves garlic, minced
· 1/4 cup pine nuts
· 1/4 cup raisins
· 1 lb fresh spinach
· Salt and pepper to taste

INSTRUCTIONS:

1 Heat olive oil in skillet.
2 Toast pine nuts until golden brown; set aside.
3 Sauté minced garlic until fragrant.
4 Add fresh spinach; cook until wilted.
5 Stir in raisins and toasted pine nuts.
6 Season with salt and pepper.
7 Serve hot.

NUTRITIONAL FACTS (PER SERVING): *Calories: 150, Carbohydrates: 10g, Protein: 4g, Fat: 10g, Fiber: 4g*

FUN FACTS AND HEALTH BENEFIT:

Spinach was originally native to Persia (modern-day Iran) before spreading to Europe and beyond.

Spinach is packed with vitamins, minerals, and antioxidants, supporting eye health and reducing oxidative stress.

Levantine Muhammara

V | GF

PREP TIME 15 MIN   **COOK TIME** 10 MIN   **SERVINGS** 2

INGREDIENTS:

- 2 large red bell peppers,
- 1 cup walnuts, toasted
- 1/4 cup fine breadcrumbs
- 2 tbsp pomegranate molasses /dried cranberries or raisins
- 1 tbsp lemon juice
- 2 cloves garlic
- 1 tsp ground cumin
- 1 tsp smoked paprika
- 1/2 tsp cayenne pepper
- 2 tbsp olive oil

INSTRUCTIONS:

1 Roast red bell peppers until charred, steam, peel, deseed, chop.
2 Toast walnuts until fragrant, cool.
3 Blend roasted peppers, walnuts, breadcrumbs, pomegranate molasses /dried cranberries or raisins, lemon juice, garlic, cumin, paprika, cayenne, olive oil, salt until smooth. Taste and adjust seasoning if necessary.
4 Transfer to serving dish, drizzle with olive oil, garnish with parsley.
5 Serve with pita bread, crackers, or veggies.

NUTRITIONAL FACTS (PER SERVING): *Calories: 100, Carbohydrates: 7g, Protein: 2g, Fat: 8g, Fiber: 2g*

FUN FACTS AND HEALTH BENEFIT:

"Muhammara" is derived from the Arabic word for "reddened" or "brick-colored".

Levantine Muhammara is rich in antioxidants from red peppers and walnuts, promoting heart health and reducing inflammation.

Moroccan Beet Salad

V | GF

PREP TIME 15 MIN   **COOK TIME** 0 MIN   **SERVINGS** 4

INGREDIENTS:

- 4 medium beets, peeled, and diced
- 2 oranges, peeled and segmented
- 2 tbsp chopped fresh mint
- 2 tbsp extra virgin olive oil
- 1 tbsp fresh lemon juice
- 1 tsp honey
- Salt and pepper to taste

INSTRUCTIONS:

1 Combine diced beets, orange segments, and mint in bowl.
2 Whisk olive oil, lemon juice, honey, salt, and pepper in separate bowl for dressing.
3 Pour dressing over salad. Toss until coated.
4 Let sit 10 mins to meld flavors.
5 Toss again before serving.
6 Serve chilled or room temp.

NUTRITIONAL FACTS (PER SERVING): *Calories: 80, Carbohydrates: 15g, Protein: 2g, Fat: 2g, Fiber: 4g*

FUN FACTS AND HEALTH BENEFIT:

Beets were originally grown for their leaves, which were consumed for their medicinal properties, before the root became popular.

Beets are high in folate and potassium, promoting heart health and reducing the risk of birth defects.

Zucchini Fritters

V

PREP TIME 10 MIN   **COOK TIME** 20 MIN   **SERVINGS** 4

INGREDIENTS:

- 2 medium zucchinis, grated
- 1 tsp salt
- 1/4 cup flour
- 1/4 cup feta cheese, crumbled
- 1 egg, beaten
- 2 cloves garlic, minced
- 2 tbsp fresh dill, chopped
- 2 tbsp fresh mint, chopped

INSTRUCTIONS:

1 Drain grated zucchini; mix with flour, feta, egg, garlic, dill, and mint.
2 Heat olive oil in skillet over medium heat.
3 Spoon zucchini mixture into skillet; flatten and cook until golden brown.
4 Drain on paper towels; serve hot.

NUTRITIONAL FACTS (PER SERVING): *Calories: 180, Carbohydrates:10g, Protein: 6g, Fat: 14g, Fiber: 2g*

FUN FACTS AND HEALTH BENEFIT:

Greek Kolokithokeftedes, or zucchini fritters, are a beloved appetizer or mezze dish in Greek cuisine.

They are not only delicious but also rich in vitamins, minerals, and antioxidants from the zucchini and herbs.

Stuffed Eggplant

V | GF

PREP TIME 10 MIN   **COOK TIME** 20 MIN   **SERVINGS** 4

INGREDIENTS:

- 2 medium eggplants
- 2 tbsp olive oil
- 1 onion, finely chopped
- 2 cloves garlic, minced
- 2 tomatoes, diced
- 1 green bell pepper, chopped
- 1 tsp sugar
- 1 tsp dried oregano
- Salt and pepper to taste
- Fresh parsley, chopped, for garnish

INSTRUCTIONS:

1 Cut eggplants in half, scoop out flesh, and salt lightly. Let sit for 10 mins, then pat dry.
2 Sauté onion, garlic, tomatoes, and bell pepper in olive oil until softened.
3 Season with sugar, oregano, salt, and pepper, and cook for 2 mins.
4 Spoon vegetable mixture into eggplant halves.
5 Place stuffed eggplants in skillet, add water, cover, and cook for 10-15 mins until tender.
6 Garnish with parsley and serve warm.

NUTRITIONAL FACTS (PER SERVING): *Calories: 180, Carbohydrates: 20g, Protein: 3g, Fat: 10g, Fiber: 6g*

FUN FACTS AND HEALTH BENEFIT:

Eggplants, native to India, were introduced to the Mediterranean region by Arab traders.

Eggplants are rich in fiber, vitamins, and minerals, promoting digestive health and reducing the risk of chronic diseases.

Greek Gigantes Plaki V | GF

PREP TIME 5 MIN **COOK TIME** 20 MIN **SERVINGS** 4

INGREDIENTS:

- 1 can (15 oz) giant beans (butter beans), drained and rinsed
- 2 tbsp olive oil
- 1 onion, finely
- 2 cloves garlic, minced
- 1 can (14 oz) diced tomatoes
- 1 tbsp tomato paste
- 1 tsp dried oregano
- 1 tsp dried thyme
- Salt and pepper to taste
- Fresh parsley, chopped, for garnish

INSTRUCTIONS:

1 Sauté onion and garlic in olive oil until softened.
2 Stir in diced tomatoes, tomato paste, oregano, and thyme. Simmer for 5 minutes.
3 Add drained beans, stir to coat with sauce, and simmer for 10 minutes.
4 Season with salt and pepper, garnish with parsley, and serve.

NUTRITIONAL FACTS (PER SERVING): *Calories: 250, Carbohydrates: 35g, Protein: 8g, Fat: 9g, Fiber: 10g*

FUN FACTS AND HEALTH BENEFIT:

The name "gigantes" in Greek translates to "giants", referring to the large size of the beans used in the dish.

Gigantes beans are packed with fiber, protein, and minerals, promoting digestive health and providing sustained energy.

Turkish Cauliflower Fritters V

PREP TIME 10 MIN **COOK TIME** 20 MIN **SERVINGS** 4

INGREDIENTS:

- 1 small cauliflower, grated
- 1 small onion, finely chopped
- 2 cloves garlic, minced
- 2 eggs, beaten
- 1/4 cup flour
- 1/4 cup grated Parmesan cheese
- 2 tbsp fresh parsley, chopped
- Salt and pepper to taste
- Olive oil for frying

INSTRUCTIONS:

1 Mix grated cauliflower, onion, garlic, eggs, flour, Parmesan, parsley, salt, and pepper.
2 Heat olive oil in skillet over medium heat.
3 Spoon cauliflower mixture into skillet, flatten, and cook until golden brown.
4 Drain on paper towels; serve hot.

NUTRITIONAL FACTS (PER SERVING): *Calories: 200, Carbohydrates: 10g, Protein: 8g, Fat: 14g, Fiber: 3g*

FUN FACTS AND HEALTH BENEFIT:

Turkish Cauliflower Fritters showcases the country's love for incorporating vegetables into their cuisine.

Cauliflower is low in calories and high in fiber, vitamins, and antioxidants, supporting digestion and immune health.

Greek Fava Santorinis

V | GF

PREP TIME 15 MIN **COOK TIME** 15 MIN **SERVINGS** 4

INGREDIENTS:

- 1 cup dried yellow split peas
- 1 onion, chopped
- 2 cloves garlic, minced
- 4 cups water or vegetable broth
- 2 tbsp extra virgin olive oil
- Salt and pepper to taste
- Chopped fresh parsley for garnish

INSTRUCTIONS:

1 Rinse split peas; drain.
2 Combine peas, onion, garlic, and broth in pot.
3 Bring to boil; reduce heat.
4 Simmer 15 mins until peas are soft.
5 Cool slightly. Blend until smooth.
6 Stir in olive oil, salt, and pepper.
7 Transfer to serving dish. Garnish with parsley.
8 Serve warm or room temp as appetizer or side.

NUTRITIONAL FACTS (PER SERVING): *Calories: 120, Carbohydrates: 18g, Protein: 6g, Fat: 3g, Fiber: 6g*

FUN FACTS AND HEALTH BENEFIT:

Greek Fava Santorinis is not made from fava beans but from yellow split peas.

Yellow split peas are rich in protein, fiber, and nutrients like folate and iron, supporting heart health and digestion.

Italian Eggplant Parmesan

V

PREP TIME 10 MIN **COOK TIME** 20 MIN **SERVINGS** 4

INGREDIENTS:

- 1 large eggplant, sliced into rounds
- 1 cup marinara sauce
- 1 cup mozzarella cheese, shredded
- 1/4 cup Parmesan cheese, grated
- 1/2 tsp dried oregano
- 2 tbsp olive oil
- Fresh basil for garnish

INSTRUCTIONS:

1 Preheat oven to 400°F (200°C).
2 Cook eggplant slices until golden brown.
3 Layer marinara sauce, eggplant, and cheeses in baking dish.
4 Sprinkle with oregano; bake 15-20 minutes.
5 Garnish with basil; serve hot.

NUTRITIONAL FACTS (PER SERVING): *Calories: 250, Carbohydrates: 15g, Protein: 10g, Fat: 18g, Fiber: 4g*

FUN FACTS AND HEALTH BENEFIT:

Italian Eggplant Parmesan, also known as "Melanzane alla Parmigiana," is a classic Italian dish that originated from the region of Campania.

Eggplant is rich in antioxidants and fiber, promoting heart health and aiding digestion.

Patatas Bravas

V | GF

PREP TIME 5 MIN **COOK TIME** 25 MIN **SERVINGS** 4

INGREDIENTS:

- 4 large potatoes, peeled and cubed
- 2 tbsp olive oil
- 1/2 cup tomato sauce
- 1 tsp smoked paprika
- 1/4 tsp cayenne pepper
- 1/2 cup mayonnaise
- 1 tbsp lemon juice
- Salt and pepper to taste
- Fresh parsley, chopped, for garnish

INSTRUCTIONS:

1 Preheat oven to 400°F (200°C).

2 Toss cubed potatoes with olive oil, salt, and pepper. Roast for 20 mins until golden.

3 Mix tomato sauce with smoked paprika and cayenne pepper. Mix mayonnaise with lemon juice.

4 Drizzle potatoes with tomato sauce, add lemon mayonnaise, and garnish with parsley.

NUTRITIONAL FACTS (PER SERVING): *Calories: 250, Carbohydrates: 35g, Protein: 3g, Fat: 12g, Fiber: 4g*

FUN FACTS AND HEALTH BENEFIT:

The origins of Patatas Bravas, a staple in Spanish tapas culture, are debated, with some attributing it to Madrid and others to Catalonia.

Potatoes are a good source of vitamins and minerals, while the spicy tomato sauce adds antioxidants from tomatoes.

Moroccan Carrot Salad

V | GF

PREP TIME 10 MIN **COOK TIME** 10 MIN **SERVINGS** 4

INGREDIENTS:

- 4 large carrots, peeled and sliced
- 2 tbsp harissa paste
- 2 tbsp extra virgin olive oil
- 1 tbsp lemon juice
- 2 cloves garlic, minced
- 1/4 cup chopped fresh cilantro
- 1/4 cup chopped fresh mint

INSTRUCTIONS:

1 Boil sliced carrots in salted water for 5-7 minutes until tender-crisp.

2 Drain and transfer to large bowl.

3 Whisk harissa paste, olive oil, lemon juice, garlic, salt, and pepper in small bowl for dressing.

4 Pour dressing over carrots, toss to coat.

5 Add cilantro and mint, toss again.

6 Transfer to serving dish.

7 Serve chilled or at room temperature.

NUTRITIONAL FACTS (PER SERVING): *Calories: 100, Carbohydrates: 10g, Protein: 2g, Fat: 7g, Fiber: 3g*

FUN FACTS AND HEALTH BENEFIT:

Historically, carrots were grown for their aromatic leaves and seeds, not their roots.

Carrots are rich in beta-carotene, promoting eye health and immune function.

Spanish Patatas Alioli

V | GF

PREP TIME 10 MIN   **COOK TIME** 15 MIN   **SERVINGS** 4

INGREDIENTS:

- 4 large potatoes, peeled and cut into chunks
- Salt
- 4 cloves garlic, minced
- 1 cup olive oil
- 1 tbsp lemon juice
- Fresh parsley, chopped (for garnish)

INSTRUCTIONS:

1 Boil potatoes until tender, about 10-12 mins. Drain.

2 Crush garlic with salt in a mortar until paste-like.

3 Gradually add olive oil, stirring into a thick alioli sauce.

4 Mix in lemon juice and adjust salt.

5 Coat potatoes with alioli sauce.

6 Garnish with fresh parsley. Serve.

NUTRITIONAL FACTS (PER SERVING): *Calories: 400, Carbohydrates: 30g, Protein: 3g, Fat: 30g, Fiber: 3g*

FUN FACTS AND HEALTH BENEFIT:

Patatas Alioli is a traditional Spanish dish originating from the region of Catalonia, known for its simple yet flavorful ingredients.

Potatoes are a good source of vitamin C and potassium, while olive oil in alioli provides heart-healthy monounsaturated fats.

Vegetable Moussaka

V

PREP TIME 10 MIN   **COOK TIME** 20 MIN   **SERVINGS** 4

INGREDIENTS:

- 1 large eggplant, sliced into rounds
- 2 potatoes, sliced into rounds
- 2 zucchini
- 2 tbsp olive oil
- 1 onion
- 2 cloves garlic, minced
- 1 can (14 oz) diced tomatoes
- 1 tsp dried oregano
- Salt and pepper to taste
- 1/2 cup grated Parmesan cheese

INSTRUCTIONS:

1 Preheat oven to 375°F (190°C).

2 Roast eggplant, potatoes, and zucchini with olive oil for 10 mins in preheated oven.

3 While vegetables roast, heat a pan and sauté onion and garlic for 3 minutes until softened.

4 Add diced tomatoes, oregano, salt, and pepper; simmer for 2 mins.

5 Layer roasted vegetables, tomato sauce, and Parmesan cheese in a baking dish.

6 Bake for 5 mins until cheese is melted.

7 Let cool briefly before serving.

NUTRITIONAL FACTS (PER SERVING): *Calories: 220, Carbohydrates: 30g, Protein: 6g, Fat: 10g, Fiber: 8g*

FUN FACTS AND HEALTH BENEFIT:

The word "moussaka" is derived from the Arabic word "musaqqa'a," meaning chilled. Vegetable Moussaka is a vegetarian twist on the traditional Greek dish.

Vegetable Moussaka is rich in fiber, which aids in digestion and promotes a healthy gut.

French Provencal Vegetable Tian

V | GF

PREP TIME 10 MIN **COOK TIME** 20 MIN **SERVINGS** 4

INGREDIENTS:

- 1 medium zucchini, thinly sliced
- 1 medium eggplant, thinly sliced
- 2 tomatoes, thinly sliced
- 1 small onion, thinly sliced
- 1 small onion, thinly sliced
- 2 cloves garlic, minced
- 2 tbsp olive oil
- 1 tsp dried thyme
- Fresh basil for garnish

INSTRUCTIONS:

1 Preheat oven to 400°F (200°C).
2 Layer zucchini, eggplant, tomatoes, and onion in baking dish.
3 Sprinkle minced garlic; season with thyme, salt, and pepper.
4 Drizzle with olive oil; cover with foil and bake 20 minutes.
5 Remove foil; bake 5-10 minutes until tender.
6 Garnish with basil; serve hot.

NUTRITIONAL FACTS (PER SERVING): *Calories: 150, Carbohydrates:15g, Protein: 3g, Fat: 10g, Fiber: 4g*

FUN FACTS AND HEALTH BENEFIT:

French Provencal Vegetable Tian, originating from the Provence region, derives its name from the earthenware dish traditionally used to prepare it.

Rich in vitamins, minerals, and antioxidants, the vegetables support immune function and reduce the risk of chronic diseases.

Stuffed Bell Peppers with Quinoa

V | GF

PREP TIME 10 MIN **COOK TIME** 20 MIN **SERVINGS** 4

INGREDIENTS:

- 4 bell peppers, tops cut off and seeds removed
- 1 cup quinoa
- 2 cups vegetable broth
- 1 tbsp olive oil
- 1 small onion, chopped
- 2 cloves garlic, minced
- 1 can (14 oz) diced tomatoes
- 1 cup black beans, drained and rinsed
- 1 tsp ground cumin
- 1 tsp chili powder
- Salt and pepper to taste
- Fresh cilantro for garnish

INSTRUCTIONS:

1. Simmer quinoa in vegetable broth for 12 minutes. Fluff with a fork.
2. Preheat oven to 375°F (190°C). Cut tops off peppers, remove seeds, place upright in baking dish. Drizzle with olive oil, season with salt.
3 Sauté onion and garlic until translucent. Add tomatoes, black beans, cumin, and chili powder. Cook for 2 minutes.
4 Mix quinoa into filling. Season and spoon into peppers.
5 Bake peppers for 6-8 minutes until tender and filling is heated.
6. Garnish with cilantro and serve hot.

NUTRITIONAL FACTS (PER SERVING): *Calories: 250, Carbohydrates: 45g, Protein: 8g, Fat: 7g, Fiber: 8g*

FUN FACTS AND HEALTH BENEFIT:

These stuffed bell peppers reflect Mediterranean influence by featuring quinoa, a nutritious grain-like seed that has become a staple in the region's cuisine.

This meal offers a balance of protein, fiber, and essential nutrients, making it a satisfying option for vegetarians and omnivores alike.

SPICES AND HERBS IN MEDITERRANEAN CUISINE

As you probably can tell by now, Spices and Herbs play an integral role in creating Mediterranean dishes. Not only do they enhance the flavors of a dish (often omitting the need for salt), herbs and spices have long been used for their healing properties throughout the Mediterranean coast.

To ensure your success in creating delicious yet healthy and flavorful dishes, I've prepared a 31-page bonus ebook - *Spice and Herb Essentials: A Comprehensive Guide to Enhancing Your Mediterranean Diet with Flavorful Ingredients* so you can start cooking Mediterranean meals with ease and confidence.

To get instant access go to: **https://heartbookspress.com/sciencebackedmediterranean-free-bonuses** or scan the QR Code below with your cell phone camera and tap on the link that pops up if you find that easier.

Inside this book, you will:

- Learn 10 essential Mediterranean herbs and spices: Understand their flavor profiles and healing properties and how they are used in Mediterranean cuisine
- Create your own flavorful homemade spice or herb blend

I hope this helps you lay a good foundation in making delectable Mediterranean meals as spices and herbs become the natural seasoning to flavor your dishes.

CHAPTER 11

WHOLE GRAINS, BEANS, AND PASTA

Explore the heartiness and versatility of whole grains, beans, and pasta in this chapter, where each recipe offers a delicious fusion of nutrition and flavor.

Embrace the healing grounding of Mediterranean grains where each bite is a joyful step towards a well-balanced life

TIPS:

· Experiment with different whole grains like farro, bulgur, and quinoa for added texture and nutrition.

· Don't be afraid to mix and match beans and grains for a protein-packed meal.

· Try roasting or toasting whole grains to bring out their natural sweetness.

· Use pasta as a canvas for your favorite Mediterranean sauces and ingredients!

Greek Spanakorizo V | GF

PREP TIME 10 MIN **COOK TIME** 20 MIN **SERVINGS** 4

INGREDIENTS:

- 1 cup long-grain rice
- 2 tbsp olive oil
- 1 onion, chopped
- 2 cloves garlic, minced
- 1 lb fresh spinach, chopped
- 1/4 cup fresh dill, chopped
- 1/4 cup fresh parsley, chopped
- Juice of 1 lemon
- 2 cups vegetable broth
- Salt and pepper to taste

INSTRUCTIONS:

1 Sauté onion and garlic in olive oil.
2 Add rice; cook until lightly toasted.
3 Pour in vegetable broth; simmer for 10 mins.
4 Stir in spinach, dill, and parsley; cook covered for 10 more mins.
5 Add lemon juice; season with salt and pepper.
6 Serve warm; top with crumbled feta cheese if desired.

NUTRITIONAL FACTS (PER SERVING): *Calories: 220, Carbohydrates: 38g, Protein: 6g, Fat: 6g, Fiber: 5g*

FUN FACTS AND HEALTH BENEFIT:

Spanakorizo translates to "spinach rice" in Greek and is a popular dish, especially during Lent when meat consumption is restricted.

Spinach is rich in vitamins, minerals, and antioxidants, promoting overall health and well-being.

Caprese Pasta V

PREP TIME 15 MIN **COOK TIME** 15 MIN **SERVINGS** 4

INGREDIENTS:

- 12 oz pasta (penne or spaghetti)
- 2 cups cherry tomatoes, halved
- 8 oz fresh mozzarella, diced
- 1/4 cup fresh basil leaves, chopped
- 3 tbsp extra virgin olive oil
- 2 cloves garlic, minced
- Salt and pepper to taste
- Balsamic glaze (optional, for drizzling)

INSTRUCTIONS:

1 Cook pasta for 10 minutes until al dente. Drain.
2 Sauté minced garlic for 1-2 minutes in olive oil until fragrant.
3 Add cherry tomatoes, cook for 3 minutes until softened.
4 Combine pasta with tomatoes and garlic.
5 Stir in diced mozzarella and chopped basil.
6 Season with salt and pepper.
7 Optional: Drizzle with balsamic glaze before serving.

NUTRITIONAL FACTS (PER SERVING): *Calories: 450, Carbohydrates: 50g, Protein: 18g, Fat: 20g, Fiber: 3g*

FUN FACTS AND HEALTH BENEFIT:

Caprese salad originated from the Isle of Capri in Italy and is a popular combination of tomatoes, mozzarella, and basil.

This dish provides a good balance of carbohydrates, proteins, and healthy fats from olive oil and mozzarella.

Moroccan Paella   V

PREP TIME 10 MIN   **COOK TIME** 20 MIN   **SERVINGS** 4

INGREDIENTS:

- 2 tbsp olive oil
- 1 onion, chopped
- 2 cloves garlic, chopped
- 1 red bell pepper, chopped
- 1 green bell pepper, chopped
- 1 cup long-grain rice
- 1 tsp ground turmeric
- 1 tsp ground cumin
- 1/2 tsp paprika
- 1/4 tsp saffron threads
- 4 cups chicken or vegetable broth
- 1 cup frozen peas
- 1 cup cooked chickpeas

INSTRUCTIONS:

1 Sauté onion, garlic, and bell peppers in olive oil until softened.
2 Stir in rice, turmeric, cumin, paprika, and saffron; cook for 1 minute.
3 Pour in broth, bring to a boil, then simmer covered for 10 minutes.
4 Add peas and chickpeas, cover, and cook for 5 minutes until rice is tender.
5 Garnish with parsley and serve with lemon wedges.

NUTRITIONAL FACTS (PER SERVING): *Calories: 320, Carbohydrates: 55g, Protein: 10g, Fat: 8g, Fiber: 7g*

FUN FACTS AND HEALTH BENEFIT:

Moroccan Paella originated in Spain's Valencia region, but its popularity has spread worldwide, inspiring unique regional variations like Moroccan Paella.

This dish offers a balance of protein, carbohydrates, and vegetables, providing essential nutrients for health.

Sicilian Pasta alla Norma   V

PREP TIME 10 MIN   **COOK TIME** 20 MIN   **SERVINGS** 4

INGREDIENTS:

- 8 oz pasta (such as spaghetti or penne)
- 1 large eggplant, diced
- 2 cloves garlic, minced
- 1 can (14 oz) diced tomatoes
- 2 tbsp tomato paste
- 1/4 cup grated ricotta salata cheese
- Handful of fresh basil leaves
- Salt and pepper to taste
- Olive oil for frying

INSTRUCTIONS:

1 Cook pasta until al dente; drain.
2 Heat olive oil in skillet over medium heat.
3 Fry diced eggplant until golden and tender; set aside. In same skillet, sauté garlic until fragrant.
4 Stir in diced tomatoes and tomato paste; cook 10-15 mins until thickened.
5 Season sauce with salt and pepper.
6 Add cooked pasta to skillet; toss to coat in sauce.
7 Serve pasta topped with fried eggplant, ricotta salata, and basil.

NUTRITIONAL FACTS (PER SERVING): *Calories: 300, Carbohydrates: 50g, Protein: 10g, Fat: 8g, Fiber: 6g*

FUN FACTS AND HEALTH BENEFIT:

Pasta alla Norma is a traditional Sicilian pasta dish named after the opera "Norma" by Vincenzo Bellini.

It is low in calories and rich in fiber and antioxidants, promoting heart health and digestion.

Rice and Fresh Herbs V | GF

PREP TIME 5 MIN **COOK TIME** 20 MIN **SERVINGS** 4

INGREDIENTS:

- 1 cup long-grain rice
- 2 cups water or vegetable broth
- 2 tbsp olive oil
- 1/4 cup chopped fresh parsley
- 1/4 cup chopped fresh cilantro
- 1/4 cup chopped fresh dill
- 1/4 cup chopped fresh mint
- 2 green onions, sliced
- Salt and pepper to taste
- Lemon wedges for serving

INSTRUCTIONS:

1 Boil water or broth, add rice, simmer covered for 15-20 mins.

2 Let rice sit covered for 5 mins, then fluff with fork.

3 Mix in olive oil, parsley, cilantro, dill, mint, and green onions. Season.

4 Serve warm with lemon wedges.

NUTRITIONAL FACTS (PER SERVING): *Calories: 200, Carbohydrates: 35g, Protein: 4g, Fat: 7g, Fiber: 2g*

FUN FACTS AND HEALTH BENEFIT:

Fresh herbs have been used for culinary and medicinal purposes since ancient times, prized for their aromatic qualities and health benefits.

They are rich in vitamins, minerals, and antioxidants, supporting immune function and reducing inflammation.

Moroccan Chickpea Tagine V | GF

PREP TIME 10 MIN **COOK TIME** 20 MIN **SERVINGS** 4

INGREDIENTS:

- 2 tbsp olive oil
- 1 onion, chopped
- 2 cloves garlic, minced
- 1 large carrot, sliced
- 1 red bell pepper, chopped
- 1 zucchini, chopped
- 1 can (14 oz) diced tomatoes
- 1 can (15 oz) chickpeas,
- 1/2 cup vegetable broth
- 1 tsp ground cumin
- 1 tsp ground cinnamon
- 1/2 tsp ground turmeric
- 1/2 tsp ground ginger
- Fresh cilantro

INSTRUCTIONS:

1 Sauté onion and garlic until soft.

2 Add carrot, bell pepper, and zucchini; cook until tender.

3 Stir in spices; cook until fragrant.

4 Add tomatoes, chickpeas, and broth; simmer.

5 Season with salt and pepper.

6. Garnish with cilantro; serve hot.

NUTRITIONAL FACTS (PER SERVING): *Calories: 250, Carbohydrates: 35g, Protein: 8g, Fat: 9g, Fiber: 8g*

FUN FACTS AND HEALTH BENEFIT:

Tagine cooking is named after the traditional clay pot with a conical lid used to prepare the dish.

Chickpeas are a good source of plant-based protein and fiber, aiding digestion and promoting satiety.

Pasta Pomodoro

V

PREP TIME 10 MIN **COOK TIME** 20 MIN **SERVINGS** 4

INGREDIENTS:

- 8 oz spaghetti
- 1 can (14 oz) diced tomatoes
- 1 can (14 oz) chickpeas, drained and rinsed
- 2 cloves garlic, minced
- 2 tbsp extra virgin olive oil
- 1 tsp dried oregano
- Salt and pepper to taste
- Fresh basil leaves for garnish

INSTRUCTIONS:

1 Cook spaghetti until al dente; drain and set aside.
2 Heat olive oil in skillet over medium heat.
3 Add minced garlic; cook until fragrant.
4 Stir in diced tomatoes, chickpeas, oregano, salt, and pepper. Simmer sauce 10-15 mins until flavors meld and sauce thickens slightly.
5 Add cooked pasta to skillet; toss to coat in sauce. Cook 2-3 mins to heat through.
6 Garnish with basil leaves. Serve hot as main.

NUTRITIONAL FACTS (PER SERVING): *Calories: 250, Carbohydrates: 40g, Protein: 10g, Fat: 6g, Fiber: 6g*

FUN FACTS AND HEALTH BENEFIT:

This dish is a staple in southern Italy, particularly in regions like Puglia and Sicily, where chickpeas have been a dietary mainstay since Roman times.

Chickpeas are high in protein and fiber, helping to maintain blood sugar levels and promoting satiety.

Pilaf with Nuts and Dried Fruits

V

PREP TIME 10 MIN **COOK TIME** 20 MIN **SERVINGS** 4

INGREDIENTS:

- 1 cup basmati rice
- 2 cups water or vegetable broth
- 2 tbsp butter or olive oil
- 1 small onion, chopped
- 1/4 cup chopped dried apricots
- 1/4 cup raisins
- 1/4 cup chopped almonds
- 1/4 cup chopped pistachios
- 1 tsp ground cinnamon
- 1/2 tsp ground cumin
- Fresh cilantro for garnish

INSTRUCTIONS:

1 Sauté onion in butter or olive oil until softened.
2 Toast basmati rice until lightly golden.
3 Add water or broth, bring to a boil, then simmer covered until rice is tender.
4 Stir in dried apricots, raisins, almonds, pistachios, cinnamon, and cumin. Season.
5 Let sit covered for 5 mins.
6 Fluff with fork, garnish with cilantro, and serve warm.

NUTRITIONAL FACTS (PER SERVING): *Calories: 300, Carbohydrates: 45g, Protein: 6g, Fat: 10g, Fiber: 4g*

FUN FACTS AND HEALTH BENEFIT:

Pilaf has ancient roots, originating in Persia, and has spread across the Mediterranean, with each region adding its own twist to the recipe.

This dish is packed with protein, healthy fats, and fiber promoting heart health and providing sustained energy.

Squash with Gnocchi   V

PREP TIME 10 MIN **COOK TIME** 20 MIN **SERVINGS** 4

INGREDIENTS:

- 1 lb store-bought gnocchi
- 2 cups butternut squash, peeled and cubed
- 2 tbsp olive oil
- 1 small onion, chopped
- 2 cloves garlic, minced
- 1/4 cup vegetable broth
- 1/4 cup grated Parmesan cheese
- 1/4 cup chopped fresh sage
- Salt and pepper to taste
- Fresh parsley for garnish

INSTRUCTIONS:

1 Boil gnocchi until cooked, then drain.
2 Sauté butternut squash until tender.
3 Add onion and garlic, cook until softened.
4 Combine gnocchi, squash, and broth in skillet, heat through.
5 Stir in Parmesan cheese and sage, season to taste.
6 Garnish with parsley and serve hot.

NUTRITIONAL FACTS (PER SERVING): *Calories: 350, Carbohydrates: 55g, Protein: 10g, Fat: 10g, Fiber: 6g*

FUN FACTS AND HEALTH BENEFIT:

Gnocchi, Italian dumplings made from potatoes or semolina, have been a part of Italian cuisine since Roman times.

Squash is rich in vitamins A and C, antioxidants that support immune function and skin health.

Cretan Dakos   V

PREP TIME 10 MIN **COOK TIME** 0 MIN **SERVINGS** 4

INGREDIENTS:

- 4 barley rusks (paximadi) or whole grain bread slices
- 2 ripe tomatoes, grated
- 1/2 cup crumbled feta cheese
- 1/4 cup Kalamata olives, chopped
- 2 tbsp capers, drained
- 2 tbsp extra virgin olive oil
- Salt and pepper to taste
- Fresh oregano or thyme leaves for garnish

INSTRUCTIONS:

1 Place barley rusks or bread slices on plates.
2 Spread grated tomatoes.
3 Sprinkle feta, olives, and capers.
4 Drizzle olive oil.
5 Season with salt and pepper.
6 Garnish with herbs.
7 Serve immediately.
8 Enjoy!

NUTRITIONAL FACTS (PER SERVING): *Calories: 200, Carbohydrates: 20g, Protein: 6g, Fat: 10g, Fiber: 4g*

FUN FACTS AND HEALTH BENEFIT:

Cretan Dakos is a traditional Greek dish. This dish dates back to ancient Crete, where the use of dried bread (paximadi) helped preserve food in the island's hot climate.

This dish provides heart-healthy fats and fiber, promoting cardiovascular health and aiding digestion.

Turkish Kisir

V | GF

PREP TIME 15-20 MIN **COOK TIME** 0 MIN **SERVINGS** 4

INGREDIENTS:

- 1 cup fine bulgur wheat
- 1 1/2 cups water
- 1/4 cup extra virgin olive oil
- 2 tbsp pomegranate molasses / dried cranberries or raisins
- 1 tsp ground cumin
- 1/2 tsp paprika
- 1/2 tsp cayenne
- 1 cucumber, finely diced
- 2 tomatoes, finely diced
- 1 bell pepper, finely diced
- 1/2 red onion, finely diced
- 1/4 cup chopped fresh parsley
- 1/4 cup chopped fresh mint

INSTRUCTIONS:

1 Soak bulgur in hot water 15 mins until tender.
2 Whisk olive oil, pomegranate molasses/ dried cranberries or raisins. , cumin, paprika, and cayenne. Fluff bulgur; add dressing, toss.
3 Add diced cucumber, tomatoes, bell pepper, onion, parsley, and mint. Season with salt and pepper. Toss to combine.
4 Serve room temp or chilled with lemon wedges.

NUTRITIONAL FACTS (PER SERVING): *Calories: 150, Carbohydrates: 15g, Protein: 5g, Fat: 8g, Fiber: 4g*

FUN FACTS AND HEALTH BENEFIT:

Kisir is a popular dish in Turkish cuisine, particularly in the southeastern region of Turkey, and is traditionally served during gatherings and celebrations.

Bulgur wheat is high in fiber and protein, supporting digestive health and providing sustained energy.

Mushroom Risotto

V

PREP TIME 10 MIN **COOK TIME** 20 MIN **SERVINGS** 4

INGREDIENTS:

- 1 cup Arborio rice
- 4 cups vegetable broth, warmed
- 2 tbsp olive oil
- 1 small onion, finely chopped
- 2 cloves garlic, minced
- 1 cup mushrooms, sliced
- 1/2 cup grated Parmesan cheese
- 2 tbsp butter
- Salt and pepper to taste
- Fresh parsley for garnish

INSTRUCTIONS:

1 Sauté onion and garlic until softened.
2 Cook mushrooms until browned and moisture evaporates.
3 Toast rice in skillet. Add broth gradually.
4 Cook until rice is creamy and al dente.
5 Stir in Parmesan cheese and butter, season.
6 Garnish with parsley and serve hot.

NUTRITIONAL FACTS (PER SERVING): *Calories: 400, Carbohydrates: 60g, Protein: 12g, Fat: 14g, Fiber: 4g*

FUN FACTS AND HEALTH BENEFIT:

Risotto originates from northern Italy, and is considered one of the most elegant and sophisticated Italian dishes.

Mushrooms are a good source of antioxidants, vitamins, and minerals, such as selenium and vitamin D, which support immune function and overall health.

Black Bean Stew

V | GF

PREP TIME 10 MIN **COOK TIME** 20 MIN **SERVINGS** 4

INGREDIENTS:

- 2 cans (15 oz each) black beans, drained and rinsed
- 1 tbsp olive oil
- 1 small onion, chopped
- 2 cloves garlic, minced
- 1 red bell pepper, chopped
- 1 carrot, chopped
- 1 celery stalk, chopped
- 1 can (14 oz) diced tomatoes
- 2 cups vegetable broth
- 1 tsp ground cumin
- 1 tsp smoked paprika
- 1/2 tsp chili powder
- Fresh cilantro for garnish

INSTRUCTIONS:

1 Sauté onion and garlic until softened.
2 Add bell pepper, carrot, and celery; cook until tender.
3 Stir in black beans, diced tomatoes, broth, and spices. Simmer stew for 10-15 minutes.
4 Season with salt and pepper.
5 Garnish with cilantro and serve hot.

NUTRITIONAL FACTS (PER SERVING): *Calories: 250, Carbohydrates: 40g, Protein: 12g, Fat: 6g, Fiber: 10g*

FUN FACTS AND HEALTH BENEFIT:

Black beans were introduced to the Mediterranean region from the Americas during the Columbian Exchange.

Packed with fiber, protein, and antioxidants, black beans support heart health, stabilize blood sugar, and promote digestive health.

Italian Pasta Primavera

V

PREP TIME 10 MIN **COOK TIME** 20 MIN **SERVINGS** 4

INGREDIENTS:

- 12 oz pasta (such as penne or fusilli)
- 2 tbsp olive oil
- 1 small onion, chopped
- 2 cloves garlic, minced
- 1 red bell pepper, sliced
- 1 zucchini, sliced
- 1 cup cherry tomatoes, halved
- 1 cup broccoli florets
- 1/2 cup peas (fresh or frozen)
- 1/4 cup grated Parmesan cheese
- Salt and pepper to taste
- Fresh basil for garnish

INSTRUCTIONS:

1 Cook pasta until al dente; drain.
2 Sauté onion and garlic until softened.
3 Add bell pepper, zucchini, broccoli, and peas; cook until tender.
4 Stir in cherry tomatoes; cook briefly.
5 Combine cooked pasta with vegetables; season.
6 Stir in Parmesan cheese.
7 Garnish with basil; serve hot.

NUTRITIONAL FACTS (PER SERVING): *Calories: 350, Carbohydrates: 60g, Protein: 12g, Fat: 10g, Fiber: 7g*

FUN FACTS AND HEALTH BENEFIT:

Pasta Primavera was popularized in the 1970s in New York City by Sirio Maccioni, the owner of Le Cirque restaurant, after being inspired by a dish he had in Italy.

This dish is rich in vitamins, minerals, and fiber from the abundance of vegetables, supporting overall health and well-being.

Couscous with Vegetables V

PREP TIME 10 MIN **COOK TIME** 20 MIN **SERVINGS** 4

INGREDIENTS:

- 1 cup couscous
- 1 1/2 cups vegetable broth
- 1 tbsp olive oil
- 1 onion, chopped
- 2 carrots, diced
- 1 zucchini, diced
- 1 bell pepper, diced
- 1 can (14 oz) chickpeas
- 2 cloves garlic, minced
- 1 tsp ground cumin
- 1/2 tsp coriander
- 1/2 tsp cinnamon
- Chopped parsley

INSTRUCTIONS:

1 Bring water or broth to boil in saucepan.
2 Stir in couscous, cover, remove from heat, let sit 5 mins, fluff with fork.
3 Heat olive oil in large skillet over medium heat.
4 Sauté onion, carrots, zucchini, bell pepper, and garlic until tender.
5 Stir in chickpeas, cumin, coriander, cinnamon, salt, and pepper; cook 2-3 mins.
6 Add cooked couscous to skillet; toss to combine.
7 Cook another 2-3 mins to heat through.
8 Transfer to serving dish. Garnish with parsley.

NUTRITIONAL FACTS (PER SERVING): *Calories: 200, Carbohydrates: 35g, Protein: 6g, Fat: 4g, Fiber: 6g*

FUN FACTS AND HEALTH BENEFIT:

In Morocco, couscous is often steamed in a special pot called a "couscoussier," with the process considered an art form passed down through generations.

This dish is packed with fiber, vitamins, and minerals from the couscous and vegetables, supporting digestive health.

Italian Pasta e Fagioli

PREP TIME 10 MIN **COOK TIME** 20 MIN **SERVINGS** 4

INGREDIENTS:

- 2 tbsp olive oil
- 1 onion
- 2 cloves garlic
- 2 carrots, diced
- 2 celery stalks, diced
- 1 can (14 oz) diced tomatoes
- 1 can (14 oz) cannellini beans
- 4 cups vegetable or chicken broth
- 1 cup small pasta
- 1 tsp dried oregano
- 1 tsp basil
- Grated Parmesan cheese

INSTRUCTIONS:

1 Sauté onion, garlic, carrots, and celery in olive oil until softened.
2 Stir in diced tomatoes and cannellini beans; cook for 2-3 minutes.
3 Add broth, oregano, and basil; simmer for 10 mins.
4 Cook pasta in the same pot until al dente, about 8-10 minutes.
5 Season with salt and pepper, then serve hot with fresh parsley and grated Parmesan cheese.

NUTRITIONAL FACTS (PER SERVING): *Calories: 250, Carbohydrates: 40g, Protein: 10g, Fat: 6g, Fiber: 5g*

FUN FACTS AND HEALTH BENEFIT:

Pasta e Fagioli was traditionally served as a peasant dish in Italy due to its simple and inexpensive ingredients.

This hearty dish provides a balance of carbohydrates, protein, and fiber from the pasta and beans, supporting energy levels and digestive health.

CHAPTER 12

FISH AND SEAFOOD

Dive into the Mediterranean's seafood treasures! From succulent grilled octopus to flavorful fish stews, these recipes showcase the region's love for fresh seafood.

Dive into the treasure trove of Mediterranean seafood where every dish celebrates fresh flavors from the ocean.

TIPS:

· Choose fresh and sustainable seafood for the best flavor and texture.

· Don't overcook - Mediterranean seafood is often cooked until tender but still flaky.

· Experiment with different marinades and sauces to add depth and brightness to your seafood dishes.

· Try grilling or pan-searing for a crispy crust and smoky flavor.

Garlic Lemon Salmon
GF

PREP TIME 10 MIN **COOK TIME** 15 MIN **SERVINGS** 4

INGREDIENTS:

- 4 salmon fillets
- 4 cloves garlic, minced
- 2 tbsp olive oil
- Zest and juice of 1 lemon
- Salt and pepper to taste
- Fresh parsley for garnish
- Lemon slices for serving

INSTRUCTIONS:

1 Preheat oven to 375°F (190°C), line a baking sheet with parchment paper.
2 Pat dry salmon fillets, place on prepared baking sheet.
3 Mix minced garlic, olive oil, lemon zest, lemon juice, salt, and pepper in a small bowl.
4 Spoon garlic lemon mixture over salmon, spreading evenly.
5 Bake for 12-15 minutes until salmon is cooked through and flakes easily.
6 Garnish with fresh parsley and lemon slices before serving.

NUTRITIONAL FACTS (PER SERVING): *Calories: 300, Carbohydrates: 2g, Protein: 30g, Fat: 18g, Fiber: 1g*

FUN FACTS AND HEALTH BENEFIT:

Salmon is a staple in Mediterranean cuisine, prized for its delicate flavor.

This popular fish is rich in protein, omega-3 fatty acids, and vitamins D and B12, supporting heart health and brain function.

Moroccan Fish Tagine

PREP TIME 10 MIN **COOK TIME** 15-20 MIN **SERVINGS** 4

INGREDIENTS:

- 1 lb firm white fish fillets
- 1 onion, sliced
- 2 cloves garlic
- 1 carrot, sliced
- 1 zucchini
- 1 red bell pepper, sliced
- 1 can (14 oz) diced tomatoes
- 1/2 cup fish or vegetable broth
- 1/4 cup chopped fresh cilantro
- 1 tsp ground cumin
- 1 tsp ground paprika
- 1/2 tsp ground turmeric

INSTRUCTIONS:

1 Clean and chop fish fillets, slice onion, carrot, zucchini, and red bell pepper.
2 Arrange onion slices in tagine or skillet. Layer garlic, carrot, zucchini, and bell pepper.
3 Place fish on top. Season with cumin, paprika, turmeric, salt, and pepper.
4. Pour diced tomatoes and broth over fish and vegetables. Simmer covered for 15-20 mins until fish is cooked and vegetables are tender.
5 Garnish with cilantro, and serve.

NUTRITIONAL FACTS (PER SERVING): *Calories: 280, Carbohydrates: 15g, Protein: 25g, Fat: 10g, Fiber: 5g*

FUN FACTS AND HEALTH BENEFIT:

Tagine cooking is about the social aspect of sharing a meal with loved ones. It's a symbol of hospitality and togetherness in Moroccan culture.

Fish is packed with essential nutrients like protein and omega-3 fatty acids, promoting heart health and overall well-being.

Calamari Fritti

PREP TIME 15 MIN   **COOK TIME** 10 MIN   **SERVINGS** 4

INGREDIENTS:

- 1 lb cleaned squid tubes, sliced into rings
- 1 cup all-purpose flour
- 1 tsp garlic powder
- 1 tsp paprika
- Salt and pepper to taste
- Vegetable oil for frying
- Lemon wedges for serving

INSTRUCTIONS:

1 Combine flour, garlic powder, paprika, salt, and pepper in a bowl for seasoned flour mixture.

2 Heat vegetable oil to 350°F (180°C).

3 Dredge squid rings in seasoned flour, shaking off excess.

4 Carefully add squid rings to hot oil in batches, not overcrowding.

5 Fry calamari 2-3 mins until golden and crispy.

6 Remove with slotted spoon; drain on paper towels. Season with salt while hot.

7 Serve hot with lemon wedges, marinara sauce, or aioli.

NUTRITIONAL FACTS (PER SERVING): *Calories: 200, Carbohydrates: 15g, Protein: 15g, Fat: 10g, Fiber: 1g*

FUN FACTS AND HEALTH BENEFIT:

Calamari Fritti, or fried calamari, is a popular Italian appetizer often served in Mediterranean cuisine.

Calamari is a good source of protein, vitamins, and minerals, including vitamin B12 and selenium, supporting overall health and vitality.

Grilled Sardines   GF

PREP TIME 10 MIN   **COOK TIME** 10 MIN   **SERVINGS** 4

INGREDIENTS:

- 8 whole sardines, cleaned and gutted
- 2 tbsp olive oil
- 1 lemon, sliced
- 2 cloves garlic, minced
- 1 tsp dried oregano
- Salt and pepper to taste

INSTRUCTIONS:

1 Preheat grill or grill pan to medium-high.

2 Rub sardines with olive oil, minced garlic, oregano, salt, and pepper.

3 Place lemon slices inside each sardine.

4 Grill sardines 3-4 mins on each side until cooked through and charred.

5 Remove from grill; transfer to serving platter.

6 Serve hot with extra lemon wedges.

7 Enjoy!

NUTRITIONAL FACTS (PER SERVING): *Calories: 150, Carbohydrates: 0g, Protein: 20g, Fat: 8g, Fiber: 0g*

FUN FACTS AND HEALTH BENEFIT:

Sardines have been a staple food in the Mediterranean for centuries, valued for their rich flavor and abundance of nutrients.

Sardines are rich in omega-3 fatty acids, protein, and vitamins D and B12, supporting heart health, bone health, and brain function.

Lemon-Garlic Butter Scallops

GF

PREP TIME 5 MIN **COOK TIME** 5 MIN **SERVINGS** 4

INGREDIENTS:

· 16 large scallops
· 2 tbsp unsalted butter
· 4 cloves garlic, minced
· 1 lemon, juiced
· Fresh parsley for garnish
· Salt and pepper to taste

INSTRUCTIONS:

1 Pat scallops dry and season with salt and pepper.
2 Heat butter in a skillet over medium-high heat.
3 Add minced garlic and cook for 1-2 minutes until fragrant.
4 Add scallops to the skillet, cook for 2-3 minutes on each side.
5 Squeeze lemon juice over scallops, sprinkle with parsley. Remove from heat and serve.

NUTRITIONAL FACTS (PER SERVING): *Calories: 150, Carbohydrates: 3g, Protein: 15g, Fat: 8g, Fiber: 0g*

FUN FACTS AND HEALTH BENEFIT:

Lemon-Garlic Butter Scallops are a luxurious seafood dish featuring tender scallops.

Scallops are low in calories and fat but high in protein, making them a nutritious and delicious seafood option.

Turkish Grilled Salmon Kebabs

GF

PREP TIME 15 MIN **COOK TIME** 10 MIN **SERVINGS** 4

INGREDIENTS:

· 1 lb salmon fillets, cut into cubes
· 1 red bell pepper, cut into chunks
· 1 yellow bell pepper, cut into chunks
· 1 red onion, cut into chunks
· Cherry tomatoes
· Olive oil for brushing
· Juice of 1 lemon
· Salt and pepper to taste
· Wooden or metal skewers

INSTRUCTIONS:

1 Thread salmon, bell pepper, red onion, and cherry tomatoes onto skewers.
2 Mix olive oil, lemon juice, salt, and pepper in a bowl for marinade.
3 Brush kebabs with marinade, coating evenly.
4 Grill over medium-high heat for 4-5 mins per side until salmon is cooked and vegetables are tender.
5 Serve hot.

NUTRITIONAL FACTS (PER SERVING): *Calories: 250, Carbohydrates: 10g, Protein: 20g, Fat: 12g, Fiber: 2g*

FUN FACTS AND HEALTH BENEFIT:

Kebabs are a cherished part of Turkish cuisine, with various meats and seafood being grilled and served on skewers.

Salmon is rich in omega-3 fatty acids, protein, and essential nutrients, supporting heart health and brain function.

Greek-Style Grilled Shrimp

GF

PREP TIME 15 MIN **COOK TIME** 5 MIN **SERVINGS** 4

INGREDIENTS:

- 24 large shrimp, peeled and deveined
- 2 tbsp olive oil
- 2 cloves garlic, minced
- 1 tsp dried oregano
- 1/2 tsp dried thyme
- 1/2 tsp dried rosemary
- Salt and pepper to taste
- Red pepper flakes (optional)

INSTRUCTIONS:

1 Whisk olive oil, minced garlic, dried herbs, salt, and pepper.
2 Toss shrimp in marinade, coat evenly.
3 Marinate shrimp in fridge for 15 mins to 1 hour.
4 Preheat grill or grill pan to medium-high.
5 Thread shrimp onto skewers evenly.
6 Grill skewers for 2-3 mins per side until pink.
7 Transfer to serving platter.
8 Serve hot with lemon wedges.

NUTRITIONAL FACTS (PER SERVING): *Calories: 150, Carbohydrates: 2g, Protein: 25g, Fat: 5g, Fiber: 0g*

FUN FACTS AND HEALTH BENEFIT:

Greek-Style Grilled Shrimp, or Garides Souvlaki, is a classic Greek dish where the use of garlic and Mediterranean herbs, results in a dish that's a nod to culinary voyage.

Shrimp is low in calories and fat but high in protein, making it a nutritious and satisfying seafood option.

Italian Grilled Swordfish

GF

PREP TIME 15 MIN **COOK TIME** 10 MIN **SERVINGS** 4

INGREDIENTS:

- 4 swordfish steaks
- 2 tbsp olive oil
- Zest and juice of 1 lemon
- 2 cloves garlic, minced
- 1 tbsp chopped fresh parsley
- 1 tsp chopped fresh thyme
- Salt and pepper to taste
- Lemon slices for garnish

INSTRUCTIONS:

1 Marinate swordfish in olive oil, lemon zest, lemon juice, garlic, parsley, thyme, salt, and pepper for 10-15 minutes.
2 Preheat grill to medium-high heat.
3 Grill swordfish for 4-5 minutes on each side until cooked through and grill marks appear.
4 Serve hot, garnished with lemon slices.

NUTRITIONAL FACTS (PER SERVING): *Calories: 300, Carbohydrates: 2g, Protein: 25g, Fat: 18g, Fiber: 1g*

FUN FACTS AND HEALTH BENEFIT:

Swordfish is a prized fish in Italian cuisine, often featured in traditional Sicilian dishes.

Swordfish is rich in protein, omega-3 fatty acids, and vitamins, supporting heart health and brain function.

Grilled Octopus GF

PREP TIME 10 MIN **COOK TIME** 15 MIN **SERVINGS** 4

INGREDIENTS:

- 2 lbs octopus tentacles
- 1/4 cup olive oil
- 2 cloves garlic, minced
- 2 tbsp lemon juice
- 1 tsp dried oregano
- Salt and pepper to taste
- Lemon wedges for serving

INSTRUCTIONS:

1 Preheat grill or grill pan to medium-high.
2 Whisk olive oil, minced garlic, lemon juice, oregano, salt, and pepper for marinade.
3 Brush marinade over octopus tentacles.
4 Grill octopus 5-7 mins each side until charred.
5 Remove from grill; let rest.
6 Slice into bite-sized pieces.
7 Serve hot with lemon wedges.
8 Enjoy!

NUTRITIONAL FACTS (PER SERVING): *Calories: 150, Carbohydrates: 0g, Protein: 25g, Fat: 5g, Fiber: 0g*

FUN FACTS AND HEALTH BENEFIT:

Octopus has been a staple in Mediterranean cuisine for centuries, with coastal communities mastering the art of cooking this unique ingredient.

It is low in fat and calories but rich in protein, vitamins, and minerals, including iron and selenium, supporting muscle health and immunity.

Mussels Marinara

PREP TIME 10 MIN **COOK TIME** 15 MIN **SERVINGS** 4

INGREDIENTS:

- 2 lbs fresh mussels, cleaned and debearded
- 2 tbsp olive oil
- 2 cloves garlic, minced
- 1/2 cup dry white wine
- 1 can (14 oz) crushed tomatoes
- 1 tsp dried oregano
- 1/2 tsp red pepper flakes
- Fresh parsley for garnish

INSTRUCTIONS:

1 Heat olive oil in skillet over medium heat.
2 Add minced garlic, cook until fragrant.
3 Add cleaned mussels to skillet.
4. Pour white wine over mussels, cover with lid.
5 Cook 5-7 minutes until mussels open.
6 Stir in crushed tomatoes, oregano, red pepper flakes, salt, and pepper.
7 Cook 5 minutes to blend flavors.
8 Remove from heat, garnish with parsley.
9 Serve hot, with crusty bread.

NUTRITIONAL FACTS (PER SERVING): *Calories: 200, Carbohydrates: 10g, Protein: 20g, Fat: 8g, Fiber: 2g*

FUN FACTS AND HEALTH BENEFIT:

Mussels are a staple in Italian coastal cuisine and have been enjoyed for centuries, with recipes varying from region to region.

Mussels are rich in protein, vitamins, and minerals, including iron and zinc, supporting immune function and overall health.

Lebanese Grilled Prawns

GF

PREP TIME 15 MIN   **COOK TIME** 6 MIN   **SERVINGS** 4

INGREDIENTS:

- *1 lb large prawns, peeled and deveined*
- *3 tbsp olive oil*
- *Zest and juice of 1 lemon*
- *4 cloves garlic, minced*
- *1 tsp ground cumin*
- *1/2 tsp paprika*
- *Salt and pepper to taste*
- *Chopped fresh parsley for garnish*
- *Lemon wedges for serving*

INSTRUCTIONS:

1 Marinate prawns in olive oil, lemon zest, lemon juice, garlic, cumin, paprika, salt, and pepper for 15-30 minutes.
2 Preheat grill to medium-high heat.
3 Thread prawns onto skewers.
4 Grill skewers for 2-3 minutes on each side until pink and opaque.
5 Transfer to a serving platter, garnish with parsley, and serve hot with lemon wedges.

NUTRITIONAL FACTS (PER SERVING): *Calories: 300, Carbohydrates: 3g, Protein: 25g, Fat: 10g, Fiber: 1g*

FUN FACTS AND HEALTH BENEFIT:

Lebanon's coastal location has influenced its cuisine, with seafood dishes like grilled prawns being popular along the Mediterranean coast.

Prawns are low in fat and calories but rich in protein, vitamins, and minerals, supporting muscle health and overall well-being.

Grilled Branzino

GF

PREP TIME 10 MIN   **COOK TIME** 10 MIN   **SERVINGS** 4

INGREDIENTS:

- *4 whole Branzino, cleaned and gutted*
- *2 tbsp olive oil*
- *2 cloves garlic, minced*
- *1 lemon, sliced Fresh herbs (such as rosemary or thyme)*
- *Salt and pepper to taste*
- *Lemon wedges for serving*

INSTRUCTIONS:

1 Preheat grill or grill pan to medium-high heat.
2 Rinse and pat dry Branzino.
3 Rub Branzino with olive oil and season with minced garlic, salt, and pepper.
4 Stuff cavity with lemon slices and herbs.
5 Grill Branzino for 5-6 minutes per side until crispy and flaky.
6 Transfer to a serving platter and garnish with rosemary or thyme.
7 Serve hot with lemon wedges.

NUTRITIONAL FACTS (PER SERVING): *Calories: 200, Carbohydrates: 0g, Protein: 25g, Fat: 10g, Fiber: 0g*

FUN FACTS AND HEALTH BENEFIT:

Branzino, also known as European sea bass, is a popular Mediterranean fish prized for its delicate flavor and tender texture.

It is a lean source of protein and essential nutrients such as omega-3 fatty acids, vitamins, and minerals.

Quick Bouillabaisse

PREP TIME 10 MIN **COOK TIME** 20 MIN **SERVINGS** 4

INGREDIENTS:

- 1 lb mixed fish and seafood cleaned and prepared
- 2 tbsp olive oil
- 1 onion chopped
- 2 cloves garlic
- 1 fennel bulb
- 1 carrot, sliced
- 1 celery stalk
- 1 can (14 oz) diced tomatoes
- 4 cups fish or seafood broth
- 1/2 cup white wine
- 1 bay leaf
- Parsley for garnish

INSTRUCTIONS:

1. Clean and prepare seafood. Heat olive oil, sauté onion and garlic.
2. Add sliced fennel, carrot, and celery; cook until softened.
3. Stir in tomatoes, broth, white wine, and bay leaf. Simmer 10 mins.
4. Add seafood, cover, and simmer 5-7 mins until cooked. Season with salt and pepper.
5. Serve hot, garnished with parsley.

NUTRITIONAL FACTS (PER SERVING): *Calories: 300, Carbohydrates: 20g, Protein: 25g, Fat: 12g, Fiber: 4g*

FUN FACTS AND HEALTH BENEFIT:

Bouillabaisse originated in the port city of Marseille, where fishermen would make this stew using the catch of the day.

This hearty soup is rich in lean protein, vitamins, and minerals from the seafood and vegetables, supporting heart health and providing essential nutrients.

Tuna Carpaccio   GF

PREP TIME 10 MIN **COOK TIME** 0 MIN **SERVINGS** 4

INGREDIENTS:

- 8 oz sushi-grade tuna, thinly sliced
- 2 tbsp extra virgin olive oil
- 1 tbsp lemon juice
- 1 tsp Dijon mustard
- 1 tsp capers, drained
- 1 tsp finely chopped fresh parsley
- Salt and pepper to taste
- Arugula or mixed greens for serving

INSTRUCTIONS:

1. Arrange tuna slices on plates.
2. Whisk olive oil, lemon juice, mustard, capers, parsley, salt, and pepper for dressing.
3. Drizzle dressing over tuna.
4. Marinate 5-10 mins.
5. Garnish with arugula or mixed greens.
6. Serve cold as appetizer.
7. Enjoy!

NUTRITIONAL FACTS (PER SERVING): *Calories: 150, Carbohydrates: 0g, Protein: 15g, Fat: 10g, Fiber: 0g*

FUN FACTS AND HEALTH BENEFIT:

Carpaccio, originally made with thinly sliced beef, was invented in Venice, Italy, in the 1950s by Giuseppe Cipriani, the founder of Harry's Bar.

Tuna is rich in protein, omega-3 fatty acids, and vitamins, supporting heart health and providing essential nutrients.

Baked Red Snapper GF

PREP TIME 15 MIN **COOK TIME** 15 MIN **SERVINGS** 4

INGREDIENTS:

· 4 whole red snapper, cleaned and gutted
· 8 anchovy fillets
· 4 cloves garlic, minced
· 2 tbsp olive oil
· 1 lemon, sliced
· Fresh parsley for garnish
· Salt and pepper to taste

INSTRUCTIONS:

1 Preheat oven to 375°F (190°C).
2 Rinse and pat dry red snapper.
3 Make diagonal cuts on both sides.
4 Stuff with anchovy fillets, minced garlic, and lemon slices.
5 Drizzle with olive oil, season with salt and pepper. Place in a baking dish.
6 Bake for 15 minutes until cooked through.
7 Let cool slightly, garnish with parsley.
8 Serve hot with lemon wedges.

NUTRITIONAL FACTS (PER SERVING): *Calories: 200, Carbohydrates: 2g, Protein: 25g, Fat: 8g, Fiber: 1g*

FUN FACTS AND HEALTH BENEFIT:

Red snapper is a popular fish in many cuisines around the world and is prized for its firm texture and sweet flavor.

It is a lean source of protein and essential nutrients such as vitamins B12 and D, selenium, and omega-3 fatty acids.

Garlic Butter Clams GF

PREP TIME 10 MIN **COOK TIME** 10 MIN **SERVINGS** 4

INGREDIENTS:

· 2 lbs fresh clams, scrubbed and cleaned
· 2 tbsp unsalted butter
· 4 cloves garlic, minced
· 2 shallots, finely chopped
· 1 cup dry white wine
· 1/4 cup chopped fresh parsley
· Salt and pepper to taste
· Lemon wedges for serving

INSTRUCTIONS:

1 Melt butter in skillet over medium heat.
2 Add garlic and shallots, cook until softened.
3 Add clams and white wine.
4 Cover and cook until clams open.
5 Season with salt and pepper.
6 Sprinkle with parsley, stir.
7 Let sit for a few minutes.
8 Serve hot with lemon wedges.
9 Enjoy!

NUTRITIONAL FACTS (PER SERVING): *Calories: 200, Carbohydrates: 10g, Protein: 15g, Fat: 8g, Fiber: 1g*

FUN FACTS AND HEALTH BENEFIT:

Clams have been harvested for centuries, with evidence of their consumption dating back to ancient times.

They are a nutritious and sustainable seafood choice, rich in protein, vitamins, and minerals such as iron and zinc.

CHAPTER 13

POULTRY AND MEAT

Immerse in a world of culinary mastery with poultry and meat dishes, where each bite tells a story of flavor, finesse, and the art of indulgence.

Discover culinary mastery in occasional poultry and meat where spices and skill transform every bite into pure delight.

TIPS:

· Utilize a mix of spices and herbs to add depth and warmth to your poultry and meat dishes.

· Experiment with various marinades and sauces to enhance flavor and moisture.

· Try incorporating chicken, lamb or beef thighs for richer, more intense flavor, but consume these meats moderately for optimal health.

· Don't forget to let your meat rest after cooking to allow the juices to redistribute, ensuring a tender and flavorful result.

Chicken with Pimentos GF

PREP TIME 10 MIN   **COOK TIME** 20 MIN   **SERVINGS** 4

INGREDIENTS:

- 4 boneless, skinless chicken breasts
- 1 tbsp olive oil
- 1 onion, thinly sliced
- 2 cloves garlic, minced
- 1 red bell pepper (pimento), sliced
- 1 can (14 oz) diced tomatoes
- 1 tsp paprika
- 1/2 tsp dried oregano
- Salt and pepper to taste
- Fresh parsley for garnish

INSTRUCTIONS:

1 Season and cook chicken until golden and cooked through, then set aside.
2 Sauté onion, garlic, and bell pepper until softened.
3 Add tomatoes, paprika, oregano, salt, and pepper. Return chicken to skillet.
4 Simmer with the lid on for 10-15 minutes.
5 Garnish with parsley and serve hot.

NUTRITIONAL FACTS (PER SERVING): *Calories: 250, Carbohydrates: 9g, Protein: 30g, Fat: 10g, Fiber: 3g*

FUN FACTS AND HEALTH BENEFIT:

Pimentos, also known as cherry peppers, are widely used in Mediterranean cuisine to add color and flavor to dishes.

Chicken is a lean source of protein, while pimentos are rich in vitamins A and C, supporting immune health and overall well-being.

Lamb Souvlaki GF

PREP TIME 20 MIN   **COOK TIME** 10 MIN   **SERVINGS** 4

INGREDIENTS:

- 1 lb lamb leg or shoulder, cut into 1-inch cubes
- 2 cloves garlic, minced
- Zest and juice of 1 lemon
- 2 tbsp olive oil
- 1 tsp dried oregano
- 1 tsp dried thyme
- Salt and pepper to taste
- Wooden skewers, soaked in water for 30 minutes

INSTRUCTIONS:

1 Make marinade with garlic, lemon zest, juice, olive oil, herbs, salt, and pepper.
2 Marinate lamb cubes for 15 minutes while preparing the grill.
3 Preheat grill to medium-high.
4 Thread lamb onto skewers.
5 Grill for 3-4 mins per side.
6 Let rest.
7 Serve with pita, tzatziki, and Greek salad. Enjoy!

NUTRITIONAL FACTS (PER SERVING): *Calories: 300, Carbohydrates: 5g, Protein: 30g, Fat: 15g, Fiber: 1g*

FUN FACTS AND HEALTH BENEFIT:

Lamb Souvlaki originated in Greece as a traditional dish of marinated and grilled meat skewers.

Lamb is a rich source of protein and essential nutrients such as iron and zinc.

Turkey Meatballs

PREP TIME 10 MIN   **COOK TIME** 20 MIN   **SERVINGS** 4

INGREDIENTS:

- 1 lb ground turkey
- 1/4 cup breadcrumbs
- 1/4 cup grated Parmesan cheese
- 1 egg
- 2 cloves garlic, minced
- 1 tsp dried oregano
- 1 tsp dried basil
- 1/2 tsp dried thyme
- Salt and pepper to taste
- Olive oil for cooking

INSTRUCTIONS:

1 Combine ground turkey, breadcrumbs, Parmesan, egg, garlic, herbs, salt, and pepper.
2 Mix well.
3 Roll into 1-inch meatballs.
4 Heat olive oil in a skillet.
5 Cook meatballs until browned and cooked through, about 4-5 mins per side.
6 Let rest for a few minutes.
7 Serve hot with sauce or sides.

NUTRITIONAL FACTS (PER SERVING): *Calories: 200, Carbohydrates: 5g, Protein: 20g, Fat: 10g, Fiber: 1g*

FUN FACTS AND HEALTH BENEFIT:

Turkey meatballs have become increasingly popular in recent years due to the growing emphasis on health-conscious eating and dietary preferences.

Turkey is a lean protein source that helps build and repair muscle tissue while being lower in saturated fat compared to beef.

Turkey Apple Salad   GF

PREP TIME 10 MIN   **COOK TIME** 0 MIN   **SERVINGS** 4

INGREDIENTS:

- 2 cups cooked turkey breast, diced
- 1 apple, diced
- 1/4 cup chopped celery
- 1/4 cup chopped walnuts
- 1/4 cup dried cranberries
- 1/4 cup Greek yogurt
- 1 tbsp lemon juice
- 1 tsp honey
- Salt and pepper to taste
- Spinach leaves for serving

INSTRUCTIONS:

1 Combine diced turkey breast, apple, celery, walnuts, and cranberries in a large bowl.
2 Make dressing by whisking together Greek yogurt, lemon juice, honey, salt, and pepper in a small bowl.
3 Pour dressing over turkey mixture, toss until coated.
4 Serve turkey apple salad on a bed of spinach leaves.

NUTRITIONAL FACTS (PER SERVING): *Calories: 300, Carbohydrates: 20g, Protein: 25g, Fat: 15g, Fiber: 4g*

FUN FACTS AND HEALTH BENEFIT:

Apples are a versatile fruit that adds sweetness and crunch to salads, while turkey provides a lean source of protein.

This salad is packed with vitamins, minerals, and antioxidants from the apples, celery, and walnuts, supporting immune health and overall well-being.

Italian Veal Saltimbocca   GF

PREP TIME 15 MIN   **COOK TIME** 10 MIN   **SERVINGS** 4

INGREDIENTS:

- 4 veal scallopini (about 4 oz each)
- slices prosciutto
- fresh sage leaves
- 1/4 cup all-purpose flour
- Salt and pepper to taste
- 2 tbsp olive oil
- 1/2 cup dry white wine
- 1/2 cup chicken broth
- 2 tbsp unsalted butter
- 1 lemon, sliced for garnish (optional)

INSTRUCTIONS:

1 Wrap veal in prosciutto and sage.
2 Season, flour, and cook in olive oil.
3 Set aside cooked veal.
4 Deglaze with white wine in skillet.
5 Add broth, simmer, then stir in butter.
6 Return veal to skillet briefly.
7 Serve hot, optionally garnished with lemon.

NUTRITIONAL FACTS (PER SERVING): *Calories: 320, Carbohydrates: 6g, Protein: 30g, Fat: 18g, Fiber: 1g*

FUN FACTS AND HEALTH BENEFIT:

"Saltimbocca" means "jump in the mouth" in Italian, referring to the dish's flavorful combination of tender veal, savory prosciutto, and aromatic sage.

It offers a lean protein source with added benefits of iron and B vitamins from veal, supporting muscle function and energy production.

Italian Chicken Piccata   GF

PREP TIME 10 MIN   **COOK TIME** 20 MIN   **SERVINGS** 4

INGREDIENTS:

- 4 boneless, skinless chicken breasts
- 1/2 cup all-purpose flour
- 2 tbsp olive oil
- 4 tbsp unsalted butter
- 1/2 cup chicken broth
- 1/4 cup fresh lemon juice
- 1/4 cup capers, drained
- 1/4 cup chopped fresh parsley

INSTRUCTIONS:

1 Pound chicken to 1/4 inch thickness, season.
2 Dredge in flour.
3 Cook in olive oil until golden brown and cooked through.
4 Make sauce with butter, chicken broth, lemon juice, and capers.
5 Return chicken to skillet, simmer.
6 Garnish with parsley and lemon slices, serve with pasta or rice.

NUTRITIONAL FACTS (PER SERVING): *Calories: 350, Carbohydrates: 10g, Protein: 30g, Fat: 20g, Fiber: 1g*

FUN FACTS AND HEALTH BENEFIT:

Italian chicken piccata is a classic dish. This dish offers a perfect balance of savory and citrusy flavors.

It offers lean protein from chicken, essential for muscle repair, paired with vitamin C-rich lemon and antioxidant-packed capers, supporting immune function and reducing inflammation.

Chicken Marbella

GF

PREP TIME 10-12 MIN   **COOK TIME** 20 MIN   **SERVINGS** 6

INGREDIENTS:

- 2.5 lbs chicken thighs bone-in, skin-on
- 1/2 cup pitted prunes
- 1/4 cup pitted green olives
- 1/4 cup capers
- 4 cloves garlic
- 2 tbsp dried oregano
- 2 tbsp red wine vinegar
- 2 tbsp olive oil
- Salt and pepper to taste
- 1/2 cup white wine
- 2 tbsp fresh parsley

INSTRUCTIONS:

1 Combine chicken, prunes, olives, capers, garlic, herbs, vinegar, and oil.
2 Marinate in fridge for 10 mins. Preheat oven to 375°F (190°C).
3 Arrange chicken in baking dish with marinade.
4 Pour white wine around chicken.
5 Bake for 18-20 mins until golden and cooked.
6 Garnish with parsley before serving.

NUTRITIONAL FACTS (PER SERVING): *Calories: 380, Carbohydrates: 12g, Protein: 30g, Fat: 22g, Fiber: 2g*

FUN FACTS AND HEALTH BENEFIT:

Chicken Marbella is known for its unique combination of sweet prunes, briny olives, and tangy capers, creating a complex flavor profile that's both savory and sweet.

Chicken Marbella provides protein and healthy fats from chicken and olives, supporting muscle and heart function.

Turkish Adana Kebabs

GF

PREP TIME 15 MIN   **COOK TIME** 10 MIN   **SERVINGS** 4

INGREDIENTS:

- 1 lb ground lamb
- 1 onion, grated
- 2 cloves garlic, minced
- 1 tbsp tomato paste
- 1 tbsp olive oil
- 1 tsp paprika
- 1 tsp cumin
- 1/2 tsp cayenne pepper (adjust to taste)
- Salt and pepper to taste

INSTRUCTIONS:

1 Mix ground lamb, grated onion, minced garlic, tomato paste, olive oil, paprika, cumin, cayenne pepper, salt, and pepper.
2 Shape mixture onto skewers.
3 Grill for 4-5 minutes on each side until cooked through.
4 Serve hot with flatbread, salad, and dipping sauce.

NUTRITIONAL FACTS (PER SERVING): *Calories: 300, Carbohydrates: 3g, Protein: 20g, Fat: 24g, Fiber: 1g*

FUN FACTS AND HEALTH BENEFIT:

Turkish Adana kebabs originated from the city of Adana and are known for their bold flavors and spicy kick.

These kebabs are a good source of protein and essential nutrients, antioxidant and anti-inflammatory properties.

Pork Tenderloin with Honey-Mustard Glaze

GF

PREP TIME 10 MIN   **COOK TIME** 20 MIN   **SERVINGS** 4

INGREDIENTS:

· 1 lb pork tenderloin
· 2 tbsp olive oil
· 1/4 cup honey
· 2 tbsp Dijon mustard
· 1 tsp apple cider vinegar
· Salt and pepper to taste
· Fresh thyme for garnish

INSTRUCTIONS:

1 Preheat oven to 375°F (190°C).
2 Season pork with salt and pepper.
3 Sear pork in an oven-safe skillet with olive oil until browned.
4 Mix honey, Dijon mustard, and apple cider vinegar for glaze.
5 Brush glaze over pork, then roast in oven for 15-20 minutes.
6 Let pork rest for 5 minutes, then slice and garnish with thyme.

NUTRITIONAL FACTS (PER SERVING): *Calories: 280, Carbohydrates: 12g, Protein: 28g, Fat: 12g, Fiber: 0g*

FUN FACTS AND HEALTH BENEFIT:

Pork tenderloin is one of the leanest cuts of pork, making it a healthier choice for meat lovers.

It is a good source of protein, B vitamins, and minerals like iron and zinc, supporting muscle health and overall well-being.

Spanish Chorizo and Potato Hash

GF

PREP TIME 10 MIN   **COOK TIME** 20 MIN   **SERVINGS** 4

INGREDIENTS:

· 4 medium potatoes, peeled and diced
· 1 onion, chopped
· 1 bell pepper, diced
· 8 oz Spanish chorizo sliced
· 2 cloves garlic, minced
· 1 tsp smoked paprika
· Salt and pepper to taste
· Olive oil for cooking
· Fresh parsley for garnish

INSTRUCTIONS:

1 Heat oil in skillet. Cook potatoes until golden and crispy (10-12 mins).
2 Add onion, bell pepper, chorizo, and garlic.
3 Cook until chorizo browns and veggies soften (5-7 mins). Stir in paprika, salt, and pepper.
4 Cook for another 2-3 mins.
5 Garnish with parsley.
6 Serve hot, with optional fried eggs.

NUTRITIONAL FACTS (PER SERVING): *Calories: 350, Carbohydrates: 25g, Protein: 15g, Fat: 20g, Fiber: 3g*

FUN FACTS AND HEALTH BENEFIT:

Spanish Chorizo and Potato Hash is a popular breakfast or brunch option in Spain.

Chorizo provides carbohydrates and dietary fiber. This hash is also a good source of protein and essential nutrients.

Tunisian Spicy Lamb Chops

GF

PREP TIME 15 MIN   **COOK TIME** 10 MIN   **SERVINGS** 4

INGREDIENTS:

- 8 lamb chops
- 2 tbsp olive oil
- 2 cloves garlic, minced
- 1 tsp paprika
- 1/2 tsp ground cumin
- 1/2 tsp ground coriander
- 1/4 tsp cayenne pepper
- Salt and pepper to taste
- Fresh mint leaves for garnish

INSTRUCTIONS:

1 Marinate lamb chops in olive oil, garlic, paprika, cumin, coriander, cayenne, salt, and pepper for 10 mins (use a warm spot to speed up marination).
2 Grill for 3-4 mins per side over medium-high heat.
3 Rest briefly, garnish with mint leaves, and serve.

NUTRITIONAL FACTS (PER SERVING): *Calories: 300, Carbohydrates: 2g, Protein: 25g, Fat: 22g, Fiber: 1g*

FUN FACTS AND HEALTH BENEFIT:

Tunisian spicy lamb chops are a tantalizing dish, known for their succulent texture and rich flavors.

It provides a protein-packed meal rich in essential nutrients like iron and zinc, promoting overall health and vitality.

Mediterranean Turkey Skillet

GF

PREP TIME 10 MIN   **COOK TIME** 15 MIN   **SERVINGS** 4

INGREDIENTS:

- 1 lb ground turkey
- 1 onion, diced
- 2 cloves garlic, minced
- 1 red bell pepper, diced
- 1 can (14 oz) diced tomatoes
- 1 tsp dried oregano
- 1 tsp dried basil
- Salt and pepper to taste
- 2 tbsp olive oil
- Fresh parsley, chopped (for garnish)

INSTRUCTIONS:

1 Heat olive oil in a skillet over medium-high heat.
2 Cook onion until translucent, 3-4 minutes.
3 Add garlic and cook for 1 minute.
4 Add ground turkey and brown.
5 Stir in bell pepper, tomatoes, oregano, basil, salt, and pepper.
6 Simmer for 10-15 minutes until pepper is tender.
7 Garnish with parsley and serve.

NUTRITIONAL FACTS (PER SERVING): *Calories: 250, Carbohydrates: 10g, Protein: 25g, Fat: 13g, Fiber: 3g*

FUN FACTS AND HEALTH BENEFIT:

Ground turkey became popular in the early 20th century as a healthier alternative to ground beef during wartime rationing.

This dish is rich in lean protein from turkey and packed with vitamins from bell peppers and tomatoes, supporting muscle growth and immune function.

Pan-Seared Duck Breast   GF

PREP TIME 10 MIN   **COOK TIME** 20 MIN   **SERVINGS** 2

INGREDIENTS:

· 2 duck breasts
· Salt and pepper to taste
· 1/2 cup fresh orange juice
· 1/4 cup chicken broth
· 1 tbsp honey
· 1 tbsp balsamic vinegar
· 1 tsp orange zest
· Fresh thyme for garnish

INSTRUCTIONS:

1 Score duck breasts and season with salt and pepper.
2 Sear duck skin-side down until crispy, then flip and cook to desired doneness.
3 Remove and let rest.
4 In the same skillet, combine orange juice, chicken broth, honey, and balsamic vinegar. Reduce until thickened, then stir in orange zest.
5 Slice duck, drizzle with sauce, and garnish with thyme before serving.

NUTRITIONAL FACTS (PER SERVING): *Calories: 350, Carbohydrates: 15g, Protein: 25g, Fat: 20g, Fiber: 0g*

FUN FACTS AND HEALTH BENEFIT:

Pan-Seared Duck Breast, a delicacy prized in French cuisine, boasts a unique layer of fat beneath its skin, rendering it rich and succulent.

It also offers iron and B vitamins essential for energy production and red blood cell formation.

Greek Chicken Gyros

PREP TIME 15 MIN   **COOK TIME** 10 MIN   **SERVINGS** 4

INGREDIENTS:

· 1 lb boneless, skinless chicken breasts, thinly sliced
· 4 pita bread rounds
· 1 cup plain Greek yogurt
· 2 tbsp olive oil
· 2 cloves garlic, minced
· 1 tsp dried oregano
· 1 tsp paprika
· 1/2 tsp ground cumin
· Salt and pepper to taste
· Tzatziki sauce
· Sliced tomatoes
· Sliced cucumbers
· Sliced onions
· Chopped parsley
· Lemon wedges

INSTRUCTIONS:

1 Marinate chicken in olive oil, garlic, oregano, paprika, cumin, salt, and pepper for 10-15 mins.
2 Cook chicken in a grill pan or skillet for 6-8 mins until browned and cooked through.
3 Warm pita bread rounds.
4 Spread Greek yogurt on pitas, top with chicken, tomatoes, cucumbers, and red onions. Drizzle with tzatziki sauce. Garnish with parsley.

NUTRITIONAL FACTS (PER SERVING): *Calories: 250, Carbohydrates: 8g, Protein: 15g, Fat: 18g, Fiber: 2g*

FUN FACTS AND HEALTH BENEFIT:

The word "gyro" comes from the Greek word "gyros," meaning "turn". This refers to the method of cooking the meat on a vertical rotisserie, which slowly turns to cook the meat evenly.

It is a balanced dish with vegetables, carbs, and protein, making it both satisfying and nutritious.

CHAPTER 14

EGG DISHES

Crack open the flavors of the Mediterranean with our egg dishes! From Turkish Menemen to Zucchini Frittata, these recipes showcase the versatility and richness of eggs in Mediterranean cuisine.

Let the humble egg take center stage in the Mediterranean pan, where simplicity meets elegance in every delightful dish.

TIPS:

· Use fresh and high-quality eggs for the best flavor and texture.

· Enhance your egg dishes with a sprinkle of smoked paprika or a drizzle of truffle oil for a gourmet touch of flavor.

· Experiment with different cooking methods such as poaching or soft-boiling to discover new textures and tastes in your egg creations.

· Try adding eggs to your favorite vegetable or meat dishes for added protein and creaminess.

Zucchini Frittata V | GF

PREP TIME 10 MIN **COOK TIME** 15 MIN **SERVINGS** 4

INGREDIENTS:

- 6 eggs
- 1 small zucchini, thinly sliced
- 1 tomato, diced
- 1/2 onion, chopped
- 2 cloves garlic, minced
- 1/4 cup grated Parmesan cheese
- 2 tbsp chopped fresh basil
- Salt and pepper to taste
- Olive oil for cooking

INSTRUCTIONS:

1 Preheat broiler.
2 Heat olive oil in skillet over medium heat.
3 Cook onion and garlic until softened (3 mins).
4 Add zucchini, cook until softened (5 mins).
5 Whisk eggs, tomato, Parmesan, basil, salt, and pepper in a bowl.
6 Pour mixture into skillet, cook until edges set but center is slightly runny (5 mins).
7 Broil in oven for 3 mins until golden and set.
8 Let cool briefly before slicing.
9 Serve hot or at room temperature.

NUTRITIONAL FACTS (PER SERVING): *Calories: 180, Carbohydrates: 8g, Protein: 12g, Fat: 10g, Fiber: 2g*

FUN FACTS AND HEALTH BENEFIT:

Frittata is an Italian egg dish similar to an omelette or crustless quiche.

Zucchini is low in calories and rich in vitamins and minerals, while tomatoes provide vitamins A and C, as well as lycopene (Heart Healthy Antioxidant).

Cypriot Eggs with Halloumi V

PREP TIME 5 MIN **COOK TIME** 15 MIN **SERVINGS** 2

INGREDIENTS:

- 4 eggs
- 1 cup diced tomatoes
- 1 cup diced halloumi cheese
- 1 tbsp olive oil
- 2 cloves garlic, minced
- 1 tsp dried oregano
- Salt and pepper to taste
- Fresh parsley for garnish

INSTRUCTIONS:

1 Dice tomatoes and halloumi cheese.
2 Heat olive oil in skillet, sauté minced garlic. Add diced tomatoes, cook until softened, about 5 mins. Add diced halloumi, cook another 2-3 mins.
3 Crack eggs into wells.
4 Cover skillet, cook eggs to desired doneness, about 5-7 mins for runny yolks.
5 Season with dried oregano, salt, and pepper.
6 Garnish with fresh parsley, serve hot.

NUTRITIONAL FACTS (PER SERVING): *Calories: 300, Carbohydrates: 7g, Protein: 19g, Fat: 22g, Fiber: 2g*

FUN FACTS AND HEALTH BENEFIT:

This is a beloved breakfast staple in Cyprus, where the salty halloumi cheese adds a unique twist to the dish,

It offers a good source of protein and calcium for bone health and muscle function, making it a satisfying and nutritious start to the day.

Poached Eggs with Yogurt V

PREP TIME 10 MIN **COOK TIME** 10 MIN **SERVINGS** 2

INGREDIENTS:

- 4 large eggs
- 1 cup plain Greek yogurt
- 2 cloves garlic, minced
- 2 tbsp butter
- 1 tsp paprika
- 1 tsp red pepper flakes (optional)
- 1 tbsp white vinegar (for poaching)
- Salt to taste
- Fresh dill or parsley, chopped (for garnish)

INSTRUCTIONS:

1 Mix yogurt with minced garlic and salt. Set aside.
2 Bring water to a simmer, add vinegar, and create a whirlpool. Poach eggs for 3-4 minutes. Drain on paper towels.
3 Melt butter, add paprika and red pepper flakes. Cook for 1-2 minutes.
4 Spread garlic yogurt on a plate, place poached eggs on top, drizzle with paprika butter.
5 Garnish with fresh dill or parsley and serve.

NUTRITIONAL FACTS (PER SERVING): *Calories: 300, Carbohydrates: 8g, Protein: 17g, Fat: 22g, Fiber: 0g*

FUN FACTS AND HEALTH BENEFIT:

Cilbir (Poached Eggs with Yogurt) is a traditional Turkish breakfast dish that dates back to the Ottoman Empire.

Greek yogurt is rich in protein and probiotics, promoting gut health and supporting muscle growth.

Turkish Menemen V | GF

PREP TIME 10 MIN **COOK TIME** 20 MIN **SERVINGS** 4

INGREDIENTS:

- 4 eggs
- 2 tomatoes, diced
- 1 onion, chopped
- 1 green bell pepper, chopped
- 2 cloves garlic, minced
- 1 tsp pul biber (Aleppo pepper) or paprika
- Salt and pepper to taste
- Olive oil for cooking

INSTRUCTIONS:

1 Heat olive oil in skillet over medium heat.
2 Add onion and garlic, cook until softened (3 mins). Add green bell pepper, cook until softened (5 mins).
3 Stir in diced tomatoes, pul biber/paprika, salt, and pepper. Cook until tomatoes break down (5 mins). Make small wells in tomato mixture, crack an egg into each.
4 Cover and cook for 5-7 mins until egg whites set but yolks are runny.
5 Remove from heat, garnish with parsley/cilantro. Serve hot with crusty bread.

NUTRITIONAL FACTS (PER SERVING): *Calories: 200, Carbohydrates: 10g, Protein: 8g, Fat: 15g, Fiber: 3g*

FUN FACTS AND HEALTH BENEFIT:

Menemen is a traditional Turkish dish often featuring Turkish spices like pul biber (Aleppo pepper) and served with crusty bread for dipping.

This is a nutrient-dense dish packed with protein, vitamins, and fiber.

Egg and Aubergine Sandwich

V

PREP TIME 5 MIN   **COOK TIME** 10 MIN   **SERVINGS** 2

INGREDIENTS:

- 4 slices of Focaccia bread
- 2 eggs
- 1 small aubergine (eggplant), sliced
- 1 tbsp olive oil
- Salt and pepper to taste
- Optional: sliced tomatoes, lettuce, hummus

INSTRUCTIONS:

1 Heat olive oil, cook sliced aubergine until golden and softened, about 4-5 mins per side. Season with salt and pepper.
2 In same skillet, cook eggs until whites set but yolks runny, about 3 mins.
3 Toast bread slices until golden brown.
4 Place aubergine slices and eggs on one bread slice, add desired toppings, top with another bread slice.
5 Serve immediately, cut sandwiches if desired.

NUTRITIONAL FACTS (PER SERVING): *Calories: 300, Carbohydrates: 20g, Protein: 12g, Fat: 18g, Fiber: 5g*

FUN FACTS AND HEALTH BENEFIT:

This popular vegetarian option harmonizes the robust flavors of grilled aubergine with the creamy texture of egg.

It offers a unique culinary experience, while also providing a nutrient-rich meal high in antioxidants and essential vitamins.

French Ratatouille Omelette

V | GF

PREP TIME 10 MIN   **COOK TIME** 20 MIN   **SERVINGS** 2

INGREDIENTS:

- 4 eggs
- 1 small onion, diced
- 1 small zucchini, diced
- 1 small eggplant (diced)
- 1 bell pepper, diced
- 2 tomatoes, diced
- 2 cloves garlic, minced
- 2 tbsp olive oil
- 1 tsp dried herbs de Provence (or dried thyme and oregano)
- Fresh parsley for garnish

INSTRUCTIONS:

1 Heat olive oil in skillet, sauté diced onion and garlic until softened.
2 Add diced zucchini, eggplant, bell pepper, and tomatoes, cook until softened and liquid evaporates, about 10-12 mins. Season with herbs, salt, and pepper.
3 Beat eggs, season with salt and pepper.
4 Pour beaten eggs into heated non-stick skillet, spoon ratatouille onto one half when edges set. Fold over, cook until fully set.
5 Slide onto plate, garnish with parsley, serve hot.

NUTRITIONAL FACTS (PER SERVING): *Calories: 250, Carbohydrates: 12g, Protein: 12g, Fat: 18g, Fiber: 4g*

FUN FACTS AND HEALTH BENEFIT:

A French ratatouille omelette combines the vibrant flavors of the traditional Provençal vegetable stew.

Packed with a medley of vegetables, it offers a rich array of vitamins, antioxidants, and fiber, making it a delicious and wholesome dish for breakfast, brunch, or dinner.

CHAPTER 15

BREADS, FLATBREADS, PIZZAS, WRAPS

Explore the artistry of dough and the versatility of Mediterranean cuisine in this chapter, where breads, flatbreads, pizzas, and wraps unite to create a symphony of flavors and textures.

In the heart of every bread, flatbread, pizza, and wrap lies a story of tradition, innovation, and the timeless joy of breaking bread together.

TIPS:

· Utilize a blend of all-purpose and bread flour to achieve the perfect balance of tenderness and crispiness in your bread.

· Experiment with grilling or baking your breads to infuse them with a smoky flavor and achieve a crispy crust.

· For a gluten-free option, consider using alternative flours such as almond flour, coconut flour, or a gluten-free all-purpose flour blend.

· Remember to consume these dishes in moderation as part of a balanced diet.

Margherita Flatbread Pizza   V

PREP TIME 10 MIN   **COOK TIME** 12 MIN   **SERVINGS** 2

INGREDIENTS:

· 2 flatbreads or naan bread
· 1 cup tomato sauce
· 1 cup shredded mozzarella cheese
· 2 ripe tomatoes, sliced
· Fresh basil leaves
· Olive oil
· Salt and pepper to taste

INSTRUCTIONS:

1 Preheat oven to 425°F (220°C).
2 Place flatbreads on baking sheet, spread tomato sauce on each.
3 Sprinkle with mozzarella, arrange tomato slices.
4 Drizzle with olive oil, season with salt and pepper. Bake 10-12 mins until cheese melts.
5 Garnish with fresh basil leaves.
6 Slice and serve hot.

NUTRITIONAL FACTS (PER SERVING): *Calories: 300, Carbohydrates: 40g, Protein: 12g, Fat: 10g, Fiber: 3g*

FUN FACTS AND HEALTH BENEFIT:

The Margherita Flatbread Pizza pays homage to its namesake, Queen Margherita of Italy.

This delicious dish offers a balance of carbohydrates, protein, and healthy fats, showcasing the essence of Mediterranean cuisine in every bite.

Za'atar Flatbread   V

PREP TIME 20 MIN   **COOK TIME** 10 MIN   **SERVINGS** 8

INGREDIENTS:

· 1 pound pizza dough, homemade or store-bought
· 1/4 cup za'atar
· 2 tbsp olive oil

INSTRUCTIONS:

1 Divide pizza dough into 8 portions, roll into circles.
2 Place on parchment-lined baking sheet.
3 Mix za'atar with olive oil to make a paste.
4 Spread za'atar paste on dough.
5 Bake for 8-10 mins until golden and crispy.
6 Cool briefly before serving.
7 Enjoy warm or at room temperature!

NUTRITIONAL FACTS (PER SERVING): *Calories: 150, Carbohydrates: 20g, Protein: 5g, Fat: 5g, Fiber: 2g*

FUN FACTS AND HEALTH BENEFIT:

Za'atar Flatbread (Lebanese Manousheh) is a popular street food in Lebanon and is often enjoyed for breakfast or as a snack.

The flat bread provides fiber and nutrients, while za'atar offers antioxidants and anti-inflammatory properties.

Greek Pita Bread V

PREP TIME 15 MIN **COOK TIME** 10 MIN **SERVINGS** 6

INGREDIENTS:

- 2 cups all-purpose flour
- 1 tsp salt
- 1 tsp sugar
- 1 tbsp olive oil
- 3/4 cup warm water
- 1 tsp active dry yeast

INSTRUCTIONS:

1. Dissolve yeast and sugar in warm water; let sit until frothy.
2. Mix flour and salt in a bowl. Add yeast mixture and olive oil; knead into dough.
3. Knead dough on floured surface for 5 mins until smooth.
4. Place dough in greased bowl, cover, let rise for 10 mins. (use a warm place to speed up the process).
5. Preheat skillet; divide dough into 6 pieces, roll into balls.
6. Roll each ball into thin circles; cook in skillet until puffed and browned.
7. Serve warm with toppings of choice.

NUTRITIONAL FACTS (PER SERVING): *Calories: 150, Carbohydrates: 30g, Protein: 4g, Fat: 2g, Fiber: 2g*

FUN FACTS AND HEALTH BENEFIT:

Pita bread is known for its pocket, perfect for stuffing with various fillings.

Greek pita bread is a good source of carbohydrates, providing quick energy for your day.

Greek-Style Grilled Pizza with Feta and Olives V

PREP TIME 15 MIN **COOK TIME** 15 MIN **SERVINGS** 4

INGREDIENTS:

- 1 store-bought pizza dough or homemade dough
- 1/2 cup crumbled feta cheese
- 1/4 cup sliced Kalamata olives
- 1/4 cup sliced red onion
- 1/4 cup chopped fresh tomatoes
- 2 tbsp chopped fresh parsley
- 2 tbsp olive oil
- Salt and pepper to taste
- Optional: additional toppings like spinach, artichokes, or roasted red peppers

INSTRUCTIONS:

1. Preheat grill to medium-high.
2. Roll out dough, oil one side, place oil-side down on grill.
3. Grill until bottom is crispy.
4. Oil top of dough, flip.
5. Add toppings quickly.
6. Close grill and cook until cheese melts.
7. Remove, sprinkle with parsley, slice, and serve.

NUTRITIONAL FACTS (PER SERVING): *Calories: 320, Carbohydrates: 30g, Protein: 10g, Fat: 18g, Fiber: 2g*

FUN FACTS AND HEALTH BENEFIT:

Greek-style grilled pizza is a delicious twist on traditional pizza, featuring Mediterranean toppings.

It offers a balance of protein, healthy fats, and antioxidants from feta cheese and olives, supporting heart health and overall well-being.

Moroccan M'smen

PREP TIME 15 MIN **COOK TIME** 15 MIN **SERVINGS** 8

INGREDIENTS:

· *2 cups all-purpose flour*
· *1/2 tsp salt*
· *1/2 cup melted butter or vegetable oil*
· *Warm water, as needed*
· *Additional melted butter or oil for frying*

INSTRUCTIONS:

1 Combine flour and salt. Gradually mix in melted butter/oil until crumbly. Slowly add warm water until dough forms. Knead until smooth.
2 Divide dough into 8 balls, brush with butter/oil, and let rest. Flatten each ball into thin shapes.
3 Fold edges towards center to form square/rectangle. Brush with butter/oil and fold again. Repeat. Heat skillet over medium heat.
4 Roll out folded dough into thin circle/rectangle.
5 Cook on skillet until golden brown on both sides. Remove and cool slightly before serving.

NUTRITIONAL FACTS (PER SERVING): *Calories: 200, Carbohydrates: 25g, Protein: 5g, Fat: 10g, Fiber: 1g*

FUN FACTS AND HEALTH BENEFIT:

M'smen, a traditional Moroccan flatbread, is known for its delicate layers achieved through a unique folding and stretching technique.

It is often made with whole wheat flour, providing fiber and nutrients like B vitamins and minerals essential for energy metabolism and overall health.

Merguez Wraps

PREP TIME 10 MIN **COOK TIME** 15 MIN **SERVINGS** 4

INGREDIENTS:

· *4 Merguez*
· *4 large flour tortillas*
· *1 cup Greek yogurt*
· *1 tbsp harissa paste*
· *1 cucumber, thinly sliced*
· *1 red onion, thinly sliced*
· *Fresh cilantro leaves*
· *Salt and pepper to taste*

INSTRUCTIONS:

1 Grill or pan-fry Merguez until cooked through and browned.
2 Mix Greek yogurt and harissa paste in a bowl, season with salt and pepper.
3 Warm flour tortillas, spread yogurt sauce down center of each.
4 Place cooked Merguez sausage on sauce.
5 Top with cucumber slices, red onion slices, and cilantro leaves.
6 Fold in sides of tortillas, roll tightly around sausage and fillings.
7 Cut wraps in half and serve immediately.

NUTRITIONAL FACTS (PER SERVING): *Calories: 400, Carbohydrates: 30g, Protein: 18g, Fat: 22g, Fiber: 2g*

FUN FACTS AND HEALTH BENEFIT:

Merguez sausage, known for its spicy kick, originates from the Maghreb region and is wrapped in the convenience of street food flair.

These wraps may provide a hearty dose of protein, essential for muscle health, and the spice blend may offer metabolism-boosting properties.

CHAPTER 16

— DESSERTS AND SWEET DISHES —

Indulge in the sweet delights of the Mediterranean! From creamy baklava to sweet orange polento cake, these recipes showcase the region's love for sweet treats.

Savor the romance of Mediterranean desserts, where every heavenly bite bursts with joy and tradition.

TIPS:

· Opt for natural sweeteners like honey or maple syrup instead of refined sugar to add sweetness to your desserts while providing additional nutrients.

· Use whole grain flours or almond flour instead of refined white flour to increase fiber content and enhance nutritional value.

· Increase the fruit content in your desserts by adding fresh or dried fruits for natural sweetness and added vitamins and minerals.

· Use Greek yogurt or coconut cream instead of heavy cream to add creaminess to desserts while reducing saturated fat content.

· Select unsweetened cocoa powder or dark chocolate chips for a rich chocolate flavor with antioxidant benefits.

Dates Stuffed with Goat Cheese

V

PREP TIME 10 MIN **COOK TIME** 0 MIN **SERVINGS** 12

INGREDIENTS:

- 12 large Medjool dates, pitted
- 1/2 cup goat cheese
- 1 tsp vanilla extract
- 1/4 cup walnut (optional)

INSTRUCTIONS:

1 Mix goat cheese with vanilla extract until smooth.
2 Fill each pitted date with goat cheese mixture.
3 Optional: add walnut.
4 Arrange on platter.
5 Serve as dessert or snack.
6 Enjoy!

NUTRITIONAL FACTS (PER SERVING): *Calories: 60, Carbohydrates: 8g, Protein: 1g, Fat: 3g, Fiber: 1g*

FUN FACTS AND HEALTH BENEFIT:

Dates stuffed with mascarpone cheese offer a delightful combination of natural sweetness and creamy texture.

This treat provides a source of fiber from dates and protein from mascarpone, contributing to satiety and potentially aiding in digestion and muscle repair.

Apricots Stuffed with Walnut

V | GF

PREP TIME 10 MIN **COOK TIME** 0 MIN **SERVINGS** 12

INGREDIENTS:

- 12 dried apricots
- 1/2 cup walnuts
- 2 tbsp honey
- 1/4 tsp almond extract
- 1/4 cup chopped pistachios (optional for garnish)

INSTRUCTIONS:

1 Soak the dried apricots in warm water for 10 minutes, then drain and pat dry.
2 Mix the honey and almond extract until smooth.
3 Make a small slit in each apricot and fill with a walnut.
4 Drizzle the honey and almond extract mixture over the filled apricots.
5 Garnish with chopped pistachios if desired.

NUTRITIONAL FACTS (PER SERVING): *Calories: 150, Carbohydrates: 38g, Protein: 1g, Fat: 0g, Fiber: 3g*

FUN FACTS AND HEALTH BENEFIT:

Apricots Stuffed Walnut make for a delectable and nutritious treat, combining the natural sweetness and vitamins of dried apricots.

This simple yet elegant dessert is both satisfying and rich in fiber and antioxidants.

Banana with Lime and Cardamom Sauce

V | GF

PREP TIME 5 MIN **COOK TIME** 0 MIN **SERVINGS** 4

INGREDIENTS:

· 4 ripe bananas, sliced
· 1/4 cup fresh lime juice
· 1/4 cup honey
· 1/2 tsp ground cardamom
· 1 tbsp lime zest
· Fresh mint leaves for garnish (optional)

INSTRUCTIONS:

1 Whisk lime juice, honey, ground cardamom, and lime zest in small bowl until well combined.
2 Arrange banana slices on serving platter, drizzle with lime and cardamom sauce.
3 Garnish with fresh mint leaves if desired. Serve immediately.

NUTRITIONAL FACTS (PER SERVING): *Calories: 150, Carbohydrates: 38g, Protein: 1g, Fat: 0g, Fiber: 3g*

FUN FACTS AND HEALTH BENEFIT:

Banana with lime and cardamom sauce is a refreshing dessert that pairs the sweetness of ripe bananas with a tangy, spiced sauce.

This dish is not only delicious but also provides vitamins, antioxidants, and digestive benefits from both the bananas and the aromatic spices.

Tahini and Date Energy Balls

V | GF

PREP TIME 10-20 MIN **COOK TIME** 0 MIN **SERVINGS** 20

INGREDIENTS:

· 1 cup pitted dates
· 1/2 cup tahini
· 1/2 cup rolled oats
· 1/4 cup chopped nuts (such as almonds or walnuts)
· 1/4 cup shredded coconut (optional)
· 1 tbsp chia seeds (optional)
· 1 tsp vanilla extract
· Pinch of salt

INSTRUCTIONS:

1 Blend dates into a thick paste.
2 Add tahini, rolled oats, chopped nuts, shredded coconut, chia seeds, vanilla extract, and a pinch of salt; blend until combined.
3 Scoop small portions and roll into 1-inch balls.
4 Optionally, refrigerate for 10 minutes to firm up.
5 Enjoy as a quick and healthy snack.

NUTRITIONAL FACTS (PER SERVING): *Calories: 80, Carbohydrates: 10g, Protein: 2g, Fat: 3g, Fiber: 2g*

FUN FACTS AND HEALTH BENEFIT:

Tahini and date energy balls, often referred to as "bliss balls," are a versatile snack.

These energy balls are a powerhouse of nutrients, boasting antioxidants from dates and healthy fats and minerals from tahini, promoting heart health.

Greek Sesame Honey Bars   V

PREP TIME 5 MIN   **COOK TIME** 10 MIN   **SERVINGS** 8

INGREDIENTS:

- 1 cup sesame seeds
- 1/2 cup honey
- 1 tbsp orange zest (optional)
- 1 tsp vanilla extract

INSTRUCTIONS:

1 Toast sesame seeds in dry skillet over medium heat until golden brown, stirring frequently, about 5 mins.

2 Heat honey in saucepan until gently boiling, reduce heat, simmer for 5 mins, stirring frequently. Add toasted sesame seeds, orange zest (if using), and vanilla extract, stir to combine.

3 Pour mixture onto parchment-lined baking sheet, spread to even thickness. Cool until pliable but not hot, then cut into bars.

NUTRITIONAL FACTS (PER SERVING): *Calories: 150, Carbohydrates: 20g, Protein: 3g, Fat: 7g, Fiber: 2g*

FUN FACTS AND HEALTH BENEFIT:

Greek sesame honey bars, known as pasteli, are a traditional sweet treat. Make this in bulk and store them for up to weeks as healthy snacks.

Rich in healthy fats, protein, and antioxidants, these bars offer a natural energy boost while satisfying sweet cravings.

Apple Slush   V | GF

PREP TIME 10 MIN   **COOK TIME** 0 MIN   **SERVINGS** 4

INGREDIENTS:

- 4 large apples, peeled, cored, and chopped
- 1 cup apple juice
- 1 tbsp lemon juice
- 1 tbsp honey (optional)
- 2 cups ice cubes

INSTRUCTIONS:

1 In a blender, combine the apples, apple juice, lemon juice, honey (if using), and ice cubes. Blend until smooth.

2 Pour into glasses and serve immediately.

NUTRITIONAL FACTS (PER SERVING): *Calories: 80, Carbohydrates: 21g, Protein: 0g, Fat: 0g, Fiber: 3g*

FUN FACTS AND HEALTH BENEFIT:

Apple slush, a refreshing beverage made by blending frozen apple slices with ice, offers a cool and fruity alternative to traditional slushies.

This icy treat retains the fiber and nutrients of apples, such as vitamin C and potassium, aiding hydration and providing a refreshing boost of natural energy.

Chia Pudding Mango Cup   V | GF

PREP TIME 15 MIN   **COOK TIME** 0 MIN   **SERVINGS** 2

INGREDIENTS:

- 1 cup coconut milk (or any milk of choice)
- 3 tbsp chia seeds
- 1 tbsp honey or maple syrup (optional, for sweetness)
- 1 ripe mango, peeled and diced
- Fresh mint leaves (for garnish)

INSTRUCTIONS:

1. Mix coconut milk, chia seeds, and honey/maple syrup (if using). Stir well.
2. Let sit for 10 minutes, then stir again. Optionally, refrigerate for 2 hours or overnight until thickened.
3. Peel and dice the mango.
4. Divide chia pudding into cups and top with diced mango.
5. Garnish with fresh mint leaves and serve chilled.

NUTRITIONAL FACTS (PER SERVING): *Calories: 200, Carbohydrates: 28g, Protein: 4g, Fat: 10g, Fiber: 6g*

FUN FACTS AND HEALTH BENEFIT:

Chia seeds can absorb up to 12 times their weight in liquid, creating a gel-like texture perfect for puddings and smoothies.

Chia seeds are packed with omega-3 fatty acids, fiber, and protein, promoting heart health and aiding digestion.

Crema Catalana   V

PREP TIME 10 MIN   **COOK TIME** 20 MIN   **SERVINGS** 4

INGREDIENTS:

- 2 cups whole milk
- 1 cinnamon stick
- Zest of 1 lemon
- 4 large egg yolks
- 1/2 cup sugar
- 2 tbsp cornstarch
- 1/4 cup sugar (for caramelizing the top)

INSTRUCTIONS:

1. Heat milk with cinnamon stick and lemon zest until simmering, then steep for 10 mins.
2. Whisk egg yolks with 1/2 cup sugar until pale, add cornstarch, mix.
3. Slowly add warm milk to egg mixture, whisking constantly. Cook until thickened.
4. Pour into ramekins, cool, then refrigerate for at least 2 hours.
5. Sprinkle sugar over each ramekin, caramelize with torch or broiler before serving.

NUTRITIONAL FACTS (PER SERVING): *Calories: 250, Carbohydrates: 38g, Protein: 6g, Fat: 9g, Fiber: 0g*

FUN FACTS AND HEALTH BENEFIT:

Crema Catalana, a classic Spanish dessert, is a rich and creamy custard topped with a caramelized sugar crust.

Though indulgent, it's a source of calcium and protein, and the hint of citrus zest provides a refreshing burst of flavor.

Moroccan Rice Pudding

V | GF

PREP TIME 5 MIN   **COOK TIME** 25 MIN   **SERVINGS** 4

INGREDIENTS:

· 1 cup short-grain rice
· 4 cups milk (or almond milk for dairy-free)
· 1/2 cup sugar
· 1/2 tsp ground cinnamon
· 1/4 tsp ground nutmeg
· 1/4 cup raisins
· 1 tsp vanilla extract
· 1 tbsp orange blossom water (optional)
· Pinch of salt
· Chopped almonds or pistachios for garnish

INSTRUCTIONS:

1 Rinse rice until clear.
2 Boil milk, add rice, simmer 20 mins.
3 Stir in sugar, cinnamon, nutmeg, raisins, vanilla, orange blossom water, salt, cook 5 mins.
4 Pour into bowls, garnish with almonds or pistachios. Serve warm or chilled.

NUTRITIONAL FACTS (PER SERVING): *Calories: 250, Carbohydrates: 50g, Protein: 6g, Fat: 4g, Fiber: 1g*

FUN FACTS AND HEALTH BENEFIT:

Moroccan rice pudding, is a beloved dessert in Moroccan cuisine. Many Mediterranean cultures have variations of the milk pudding (Greek, Spain, France etc.).

This dessert offers a comforting and satisfying treat while providing a source of carbohydrates from rice, essential for energy, and calcium from milk, which supports bone health and muscle function.

Poached Pears

V | GF

PREP TIME 5 MIN   **COOK TIME** 20 MIN   **SERVINGS** 4

INGREDIENTS:

· 4 ripe pears, peeled and cored
· 2 cups red wine (e.g., Merlot or Shiraz)
· 1/2 cup sugar
· 1 cinnamon stick
· 2 star anise
· 4 cloves
· 1 orange, zest and juice
· 1 tsp vanilla extract

INSTRUCTIONS:

1 Combine red wine, sugar, cinnamon, star anise, cloves, orange zest, and juice in saucepan. Simmer until sugar dissolves.
2 Add pears, poach until tender, about 15 mins.
3 Remove pears, boil syrup until slightly thickened, about 5 mins. Drizzle over pears. Serve warm or chilled.

NUTRITIONAL FACTS (PER SERVING): *Calories: 200, Carbohydrates: 40g, Protein: 1g, Fat: 0g, Fiber: 5g*

FUN FACTS AND HEALTH BENEFIT:

Poached pears, originally a French delicacy, have become a beloved dessert worldwide.

Poached pears offer a guilt-free dessert option, as they are naturally low in fat and cholesterol while being rich in dietary fiber, which supports digestive health and can aid in weight management.

Ricotta and Berry Parfait V | GF

PREP TIME 10 MIN **COOK TIME** 0 MIN **SERVINGS** 2

INGREDIENTS:

- 1 cup ricotta cheese
- 1 cup mixed berries (strawberries, blueberries, raspberries)
- 2 tbsp honey
- 1/2 tsp vanilla extract
- 1/4 cup granola
- Fresh mint leaves for garnish (optional)

INSTRUCTIONS:

1 Mix ricotta cheese, honey, and vanilla extract until smooth in a bowl.
2 In serving glasses, layer ricotta mixture, mixed berries, and granola.
3 Repeat layers until glasses are filled, ending with berries.
4 Garnish with fresh mint leaves if desired. Serve immediately.

NUTRITIONAL FACTS (PER SERVING): *Calories: 200, Carbohydrates: 25g, Protein: 8g, Fat: 8g, Fiber: 3g*

FUN FACTS AND HEALTH BENEFIT:

Ricotta and berry parfait, a delightful dessert originating from Italy, layers creamy ricotta cheese with fresh berries.

This parfait offers a balance of protein from ricotta cheese and vitamins, minerals, and antioxidants from berries, supporting muscle health, and providing essential nutrients for overall well-being.

Grape and Almond Smoothie V | GF

PREP TIME 5 MIN **COOK TIME** 0 MIN **SERVINGS** 2

INGREDIENTS:

- 1 cup red or green grapes
- 1/2 cup almond milk
- 1/4 cup plain Greek yogurt
- 1 tbsp almond butter
- 1 tbsp honey
- 1/2 tsp vanilla extract
- 1 cup ice cubes

INSTRUCTIONS:

1 In a blender, combine the grapes, almond milk, Greek yogurt, almond butter, honey, vanilla extract, and ice cubes. Blend until smooth.
2 Pour into glasses and serve immediately.

NUTRITIONAL FACTS (PER SERVING): *Calories: 180, Carbohydrates: 29g, Protein: 5g, Fat: 6g, Fiber: 2g*

FUN FACTS AND HEALTH BENEFIT:

Grapes, one of the oldest cultivated fruits, offer a rich source of antioxidants like resveratrol, known for its potential health benefits.

Almonds, often referred to as "the king of nuts," are packed with nutrients like vitamin E, magnesium, and fiber, making them a powerhouse ingredient in this smoothie.

Quick Baklava Bites

V

PREP TIME 10 MIN   **COOK TIME** 12 MIN   **SERVINGS** 30

INGREDIENTS:

- 1 cup chopped walnuts
- 1 cup chopped pistachios
- 1 tsp ground cinnamon
- 1/2 tsp ground cloves
- 1/4 cup maple syrup
- 1/2 cup honey
- 1/4 cup melted butter
- 1 package mini phyllo shells (about 30 shells)

INSTRUCTIONS:

1 Preheat oven to 350°F (175°C).

2 Combine chopped walnuts, pistachios, cinnamon, cloves, and maple syrup in a bowl.

3 Arrange mini phyllo shells on a baking sheet, fill each with nut mixture.

4. Drizzle honey and melted butter over filled shells.

5 Bake for 10-12 minutes until golden and crisp.

6 Let cool slightly before serving.

NUTRITIONAL FACTS (PER SERVING): *Calories: 150, Carbohydrates: 16g, Protein: 2g, Fat: 9g, Fiber: 1g*

FUN FACTS AND HEALTH BENEFIT:

Quick baklava bites, inspired by the iconic Turkish dessert, are a miniature rendition of the traditional pastry.

Despite their sweet and indulgent taste, these bites can offer a source of protein and healthy fats from nuts, along with antioxidants and anti-inflammatory properties.

Fruit Salad with Mint

V | GF

PREP TIME 10 MIN   **COOK TIME** 0 MIN   **SERVINGS** 6

INGREDIENTS:

- 2 cups diced apple
- 2 cups diced banana
- 2 cups diced pineapple
- 1 cup blueberries
- 1/4 cup fresh mint leaves, chopped
- Juice of 1 lemon
- 1 tbsp honey (optional)

INSTRUCTIONS:

1 Mix apple, banana, pineapple, and blueberries in a large bowl.

2 Drizzle lemon juice and honey over fruit, add chopped mint, toss gently.

3 Serve immediately or refrigerate until ready to serve.

NUTRITIONAL FACTS (PER SERVING): *Calories: 80, Carbohydrates: 21g, Protein: 1g, Fat: 0g, Fiber: 2g*

FUN FACTS AND HEALTH BENEFIT:

This vibrant and refreshing dessert features a mix of fresh fruits enhanced by a zesty lemon dressing and aromatic mint.

This healthy dessert is packed with vitamins, antioxidants, and hydration, making it a perfectly light and nutritious option.

Spanish Churros

V

PREP TIME 15 MIN   **COOK TIME** 15 MIN   **SERVINGS** 12

INGREDIENTS:

- 1/2 cup unsalted butter
- 1 tbsp maple syrup
- 1/4 tsp salt
- 1 cup all-purpose flour
- 2 large eggs
- Vegetable oil, for frying
- 1/2 cup maple syrup (for coating)
- 1 tsp ground cinnamon (for coating)

INSTRUCTIONS:

1 Boil water, butter, sugar, and salt. Stir in flour until dough forms and let cool slightly.
2 Beat in eggs until smooth.
3 Heat oil to 350°F (175°C) in a skillet.
4 Pipe dough into hot oil, cut into strips, and fry until golden brown.
5 Drain briefly on paper towels.
6 Roll warm churros in cinnamon-sugar mixture.
7 Serve warm and enjoy!

NUTRITIONAL FACTS (PER SERVING): *Calories: 150, Carbohydrates: 18g, Protein: 2g, Fat: 8g, Fiber: 0.5g*

FUN FACTS AND HEALTH BENEFIT:

Churros are believed to have originated in Spain and Portugal and were brought to Latin America by Spanish colonizers.

While churros are indulgent, the joy they bring can positively impact mood and relaxation, contributing to overall well-being when enjoyed in moderation.

Italian Lemon Sorbet

V | GF

PREP TIME 15 MIN   **COOK TIME** 0 MIN   **SERVINGS** 8

INGREDIENTS:

- 1 cup maple syrup
- 1 cup water
- 1 cup freshly squeezed lemon juice (about 4-6 lemons)
- Zest of 1 lemon

INSTRUCTIONS:

1 Stir maple syrup in lemon juice and zest.
2 Pour into dish, freeze.
3 Scrape and stir every 30 mins until smooth, 3-4 hours.
4 Transfer to airtight container, freeze.
5 Serve in chilled bowls or cones.
6 Enjoy!

NUTRITIONAL FACTS (PER SERVING): *Calories: 100, Carbohydrates: 25g, Protein: 0g, Fat: 0g, Fiber: 1g*

FUN FACTS AND HEALTH BENEFIT:

Lemon Sorbet is a refreshing frozen dessert that originated in Italy.

This delightful dessert is low in fat and calories, making it a healthier alternative to ice cream or gelato.

30 DAYS MEAL PLANNING
WITH SHOPPING LIST

DAY	BREAKFAST	SNACK	LUNCH	SNACK	DINNER	CALORIES (KCAL)
1	Shakshuka (300kcal)	Grape and Almond Smoothie (180kcal)	Spanish Chorizo and Avocado Salad (400kcal)	Crema Catalana (250kcal)	Garlic Lemon Salmon (300kcal)	1430
2	Frittata (250kcal)	Mediterranean Chickpea Pancakes (170kcal)	Italian Chicken Piccata (350kcal)	Poached Eggs with Yogurt (300kcal)	Moroccan Chickpea Tagine (250kcal)	1320
3	Omelette with Spinach and Feta (250 kcal)	Poached Pears (200kcal)	Sicilian Pasta alla Norma (300kcal)	Ricotta and Berry Parfait (200kcal)	Greek-style Grilled Pizza with Feta and Olives (320kcal)	1270
4	Mediterranean Diet Oatmeal (300kcal)	Pumpkin and Walnut (180kcal)	Broccoli and Almond Soup (250kcal)	Egg and Aubergine Sandwich (300)	Italian Pasta Primavera (350kcal)	1380
5	Mediterranean Breakfast Sandwich (350kcal)	Greek Dolmades (250kcal)	Green Lentil Soup (250kcal)	Moroccan Rice Pudding (250kcal)	Turkish Grilled Salmon Kebabs (250kcal)	1350
6	Greek Scrambled Eggs (240kcal)	Turkish Sigara Böreği (160kcal)	Spanish Patatas Alioli (400kcal)	Chia Pudding Mango Cup (200kcal)	Moroccan Fish Tagine + Tuscan Sun Dip (340kcal)	1340
7	Avocado Toast + Greek Yogurt Fage (125g) (438kcal)	Quick Zucchini Stuffed Boats (210kcal)	Spanish Chorizo and Potato Hash (350kcal)	Za'atar Flatbread + Apricots Stuffed with Walnut (300kcal)	Lamb Souvlaki (300kcal)	1598
8	Spanish Potato Omelette (300kcal)	Turkish Lahmacun (250kcal)	Moroccan Carrot and Chickpea Salad (300kcal)	Grilled Octopus (150kcal)	Merguez Wraps (400kcal)	1400
9	Avocado Toast + Labneh (310kcal)	Moroccan Baked Brie (150kcal)	Pilaf with Nuts and Dried Fruits (300)	Tuna Carpaccio (150kcal)	Pan-Seared Duck Breast (350kcal)	1260
10	Mediterranean Diet Oatmeal (300kcal)	Espinacas con garbanzos (180kcal)	Squash with Gnocchi (350kcal)	Turkey Meatballs (200kcal)	Turkish Adana Kebabs (300kcal)	1330
11	Bruschetta with Tomato and Basil + Greek Yogurt Fage (338kcal)	Garlic Shrimp (180kcal)	Tunisian Spicy Lamb Chops (300kcal)	Spanish Chorizo and Potato Hash (350kcal)	Moroccan Paella (320)	1488

12	Mediterranean Chickpea Pancakes + Grape and Almond Smoothie (350kcal)	Greek-Style Grilled Shrimp (150kcal)	Mushroom Risotto (400kcal)	Turkey Apple Salad (300kcal)	Lebanese Grilled Prawns (300kcal)	1500
13	Cypriot Eggs with Halloumi (300kcal)	Moroccan M'smen (200kcal)	Moroccan Beet Salad + Black Bean Stew (330kcal)	Banana with Lime and Cardamom Sauce (150kcal)	Italian Veal Saltimbocca (320kcal)	1300
14	Cretan Dakos+ Apple Slush (280kcal)	Greek Sesame Honey Bars (150kcal)	Salad Nicoise (350kcal)	Grilled Octopus (150kcal)	Chicken Marbella (380kcal)	1310
15	Poached Eggs with Yogurt (300kcal)	Dates Stuffed with goat Cheese + Grape and Almond Smoothie (240kcal)	Quick Bouillabaisse (300kcal)	Crema Catalana (250kcal)	Margherita Flatbread Pizza (300kcal)	1390
16	Shakshuka (300kcal)	Greek Tzatziki with Pita Bread (150kcal)	Mediterranean Turkey Skillet (250kcal)	Moroccan Rice Pudding (250kcal)	Pork Tenderloin with Honey-Mustard Glaze + Tuscan Sun Dip (340kcal)	1290
17	Spanish Potato Omelette (300kcal)	Caprese Skewers (120kcal)	Rice and Fresh Herbs + Turkey Meatballs (400kcal)	Quick Baklava Bites (150kcal)	Pan-Seared Duck Breast (350kcal)	1320
18	French Ratatouille Omelette (250kcal)	Turkish Lahmacun (250kcal)	Merguez Wraps (400kcal)	Chia Pudding Mango Cup (200kcal)	French Soupe au Pistou + Lemon-Garlic Butter Scallops (400kcal)	1500
19	Mediterranean Diet Oatmeal (300kcal)	Apricots Stuffed with Walnut (150kcal)	Sicilian Pasta alla Norma (300kcal)	Greek Spanakorizo (220kcal)	Mushroom Risotto (400kcal)	1370
20	Egg and Aubergine Sandwich (300kcal)	Poached Pears (200kcal)	Greek-Style Grilled Pizza with Feta and Olives (320kcal)	Vegetable Moussaka (220kcal)	Italian Pasta Primavera (350kcal)	1390
21	Greek Scrambled Eggs (Strapatsada) (240kcal)	Greek Dolmades (250kcal)	Moroccan Paella (320kcal)	Squash with Gnocchi (350kcal)	Turkish Grilled Salmon Kebabs + Hummus with Crudité Platter (350kcal)	1510
22	Frittata (250kcal)	Crema Catalana (250kcal)	Baked Red Snapper + Greek Olive Essence (280kcal)	Calamari Fritti (200kcal)	Moroccan Paella (320kcal)	1300
23	Spanish Chorizo and Potato Hash (350kcal)	Spanish Churros (150kcal)	Lamb Souvlaki (300kcal)	Moroccan Carrot and Chickpea Salad (300kcal)	Quick Bouillabaisse (300kcal)	1400
24	Mediterranean Turkey Skillet (250kcal)	Ricotta and Berry Parfait (200kcal)	Tunisian Spicy Lamb Chops (300kcal)	Turkey Apple Salad (300kcal)	Pilaf with Nuts and Dried Fruits (300kcal)	1350

25	Za'atar Flatbread + Grape and Almond Smoothie (330kcal)	Ricotta and Berry Parfait (200kcal)	Italian Grilled Swordfish (300kcal)	Moroccan M'smen (200kcal)	Greek-Style Grilled Pizza with Feta and Olives (320kcal)	1350
26	Turkish Ezme + Chia Pudding Mango Cup (300kcal)	Grape and Almond Smoothie (180kcal)	Spanish Patatas Alioli (400kcal)	Banana with Lime and Cardamom Sauce (150kcal)	Moroccan Fish Tagine (280kcal)	1310
27	Cypriot Eggs with Halloumi (300kcal)	Moroccan Rice Pudding (250kcal)	Patatas Bravas + Greek Fava Santorinis (370kcal)	Pasta Pomodoro (250kcal)	Italian Chicken Piccata (350kcal)	1520
28	Mediterranean Breakfast Sandwich (350kcal)	Poached Pears (200kcal)	Turkish Eggplant Salad + Pork Tenderloin with Honey-Mustard Glaze (370kcal)	Stuffed Bell Peppers with Quinoa (250kcal)	Merguez Wraps (400kcal)	1570
29	Bruschetta with Tomato and Basil + Greek Yogurt Fage (338kcal)	Garlic Shrimp (180kcal)	Tunisian Spicy Lamb Chops (300kcal)	Spanish Chorizo and Potato Hash (350kcal)	Moroccan Paella (320)	1488
30	Greek Pita Bread + Grape and Almond Smoothie (350kcal)	Italian Lemon Sorbet (100kcal)	Greek Chicken Gyros (250kcal)	Italian Chicken Piccata (350kcal)	Turkey Meatballs + Zucchini with Moroccan Spices (320kcal)	1370

To help you shop better with the above 30-day meal plan, I've included detailed weekly shopping lists with quantities to purchase per week in a digital booklet.

Please go to: https://heartbookspress.com/sciencebackedmediterranean-free-bonuses to download it or scan the QR Code below with your cell phone camera and tap on the link that pops up if you find that easier.

CONCLUSION

As we wrap up our Mediterranean culinary odyssey, I want to extend my heartfelt appreciation for welcoming me into your kitchen and your life. The Mediterranean diet, steeped in centuries of tradition and well-being, transcends mere food—it's a lifestyle, a celebration of vitality, and a rediscovery of the joys found in nourishing, flavorful meals.

Each step you take towards embracing this healthier lifestyle is a triumph, no matter how small. Whether you've fully embraced the Mediterranean way of eating or are gradually integrating recipes into your routine, every effort contributes to a better you.

This cookbook was crafted with love and care, driven by a sincere desire to offer not only delicious but also health-enhancing meals. I hope that as you've explored each recipe, you've not only relished their flavors but also sensed the dedication and enthusiasm behind their creation.

In times of challenge, return to these pages, draw inspiration from the vibrant photographs, and recall the reasons you embarked on this journey. Health, vitality, and the simple joy of eating well are invaluable gifts that enrich our lives.

Thank you for joining me on this Mediterranean adventure. May your days be filled with delightful meals, moments of joy, and the deep satisfaction that comes from nurturing yourself.

To Good Health and Delicious Memories

Made in United States
Troutdale, OR
01/03/2025

27580328R00064